Andrew M. Greeley

A PIECE OF
MY MIND . . .

On Just About Everything

IMAGE BOOKS
A Division of Doubleday & Company, Inc.
Garden City, New York
1985

Image Books edition published September 1985 by special arrangement with Doubleday & Company, Inc.

Library of Congress Cataloging in Publication Data

Greeley, Andrew M., 1928–
   A piece of my mind . . . on just about everything.

  "The articles in this book originally appeared in
various newspapers across the country . . . between
1980 and 1982"—Verso t.p.

   1. Christianity—20th century—Addresses, essays,
lectures.   2. United States—Civilization—20th century—
Addresses, essays, lectures.   3. Moral conditions.
4. Catholic Church—History—20th century—Addresses,
essays, lectures.   I. Title.
BR479.G74   1983   209'.73
ISBN 0-385-23237-3
Library of Congress Catalog Card Number 82–45966

Contents

POLITICS 41

RELIGION 61

CHURCH 133

YOUTH 173

THE POPE 195

AND A FEW OTHER THINGS BESIDES 213

8   *Contents*

Introduction

Occasionally someone who has just met me will make the totally unfounded charge that I am pleasant or even charming, "not at all like I thought you'd be from reading your column."

I vigorously defend myself against such accusations. I am indeed perverse, contentious, difficult, unpredictable, combative, opinionated, pugnacious, angry and outrageous.

When I am wearing my columnist's hat.

And in that role all the above adjectives are flattery.

When I was a boy my father's business brought us to Mississippi often. In those days the Jackson *Daily News* featured on its front page a columnist named Fred Sullins. He was read every morning before anything else in the newspaper because people wanted to see what "that SOB Fred said today."

A kind of Mike Royko of the South.

It has seemed to me ever since that Sullins had grasped what writing columns was all about, as Royko has today. The columnist challenges, disconcerts, stimulates, outrages, entertains and, above all, forces you to think. A good columnist is one whom people read before anything else in the paper because they want to see what the so-and-so is up to now.

And a great columnist like Royko can be so popular that he will sustain an otherwise terrible paper from collapse. Even those who don't like what he has to say will read him if only because they enjoy being made angry by him.

So a columnist does not seek to edify or to instruct or to reassure or to win agreement. He seeks rather to stir things up and challenge your preconceptions and prejudices.

Many of the more distinguished national columnists, it seems to me, commit the unpardonable professional crime of predictability. You know where they will stand on every issue. And, having read the first sentence of a given column, you can be certain what the rest of it will say.

They may be weighty and important men, heaven knows. But predictability is only one step away from dullness.

So, when the late Jim Andrews, God be good to him, asked me to expand my once-a-week Catholic column to two columns a week for the secular press (it somehow became three in addition to the weekly Catholic column), I resolved to try to avoid predictability and dullness even if it meant that the columns would be outrageous, contentious, perverse and all those other things.

It was not very difficult to don the hat.

I am dismayed every time someone says, "I don't always agree with you" (a form of demeaning and patronizing comment of which priests are especially fond). Who the hell wants agreement?

Or writes because he expects it?

I mean, they have the right to be wrong.

If readers want to judge my personality and character by this collection, that's their right, having paid their money for the book.

But they should no more expect self-revelation than they should expect edification or instruction or a desperate need for agreement.

If they want self-revelation, if they want to know "what he's *really* like (and I can't imagine why people care about that), they should try my fiction or my poetry.

As for the columnist's hat, to paraphrase Belloc slightly,

> May it be said
> When I am dead
> His sins were scarlet
> His columns were read.

ANDREW M. GREELEY
September 23, 1982

WOMEN

What does a priest know about women?

More than most other men because we know more women more intimately than do most men, except psychiatrists and other therapy types.

And some of us know more about them than their husbands do. You may sleep with a woman for decades and not know her at all and not understand other women through her.

And you may be a celibate and, precisely because of the perspective that your distance gives you, understand women very well indeed.

Which means that you know how little you understand them.

Whether I understand women or not, however, is beside the point of these columns.

The point is I like them, on the whole more than I like men.

I am an incurable male chauvinist by the standards of the radical feminists. I admire women's bodies greatly.

I also enjoy their minds.

And their attention and their affection and their concern.

I like them strong, I like them smart, I like them pretty (and that need have little to do with age).

And, God help me, I like them Irish.

I like them a lot.

So that's why I write about them.

Why These Bouts
of Depression?

My God, it's difficult to be a woman!

That sentence is a statement, an exclamation and a prayer.

It's difficult to be a man too, but the difficulties are different. One of the big differences is that few of us men, even the most tender and sensitive, are very good at comprehending emotionally and intellectually the difficulties of being a woman, much less responding with sympathy and skill. Most women, on the other hand, have known since childhood just how to respond to our difficulties and do so spontaneously and naturally, sometimes even when they don't want to.

A woman colleague spoke to me recently about a hotel at which she stays when traveling to a certain city. The two competent and friendly plainclothes cops in the lobby make her feel safer there than she would at other hotels. A man would hardly notice the cops. He wouldn't have to.

Actress Nancy Allen, defending the violence in *Dressed to Kill*, said that anything that warned women to stay out of empty elevators was good. A man would not think of hesitating to enter an empty elevator in a plush apartment building. He wouldn't have to.

Maggie Schaff, in her new book, *Unfinished Business*, considers the question of why so many more women than men are plagued with depression, neuroses and psychoses. Her conclusion: Men become depressed at loss or the prospect of loss in the success game. Women become depressed at loss or the prospect of loss of the loved Other. Ms. Schaff might add that women know how to respond to men's depression while most men do not notice women's depression or understand what women have to be depressed about.

According to Ms. Schaff, human babies come into the world strongly "prepackaged" to form a love bond with the caring Other; the advance programming, however, is notably stronger in girl babies. From the very beginning, then, on the average, the love bond is more important to women (as early as three days after birth).

Furthermore, they learn very early that masculine traits of self-sufficiency and independence are the true proof of human worth. Hence, they are told that the very qualities that make them different also make them inferior. If they want to be valued they must acquire the self-sufficiency of men; yet they must also maintain the affectionate characteristics of women. They must be men and women at the same time.

Men must only be men.

Contemporary feminism makes things worse for women. Feminists insist vigorously on the need for self-sufficiency and independence to overcome depression. Traditionalists argue that, to the contrary, career women will be more depressed because they are cut off from the "natural" sources of affection. Ms. Schaff points out the devastating fact that both career women and non-career women are equally prone to depression.

Oriented surely by culture and probably by biology to invest more of herself in human affection, the woman hears both from the traditionalist and the feminist that the affection orientation marks her as an inferior human. The traditionalist says that she will find happiness by dutifully accepting the inferiority of the affectionate, while the feminist says she will find happiness by escaping from the affectionate.

Very few people seem willing to assert what I believe: Affection is far more human and far more admirable than achievement. I'm not very good at it, God knows, but I still think it is superior.

Escape for women, then, is not to be found in a return to the biological or in a revolt against affection. It is to be found rather in a reorientation of social values so that affection is at least as important as achievement and love bonds are as at least as important as independence. Such values in turn demand a restructuring of social order so that it becomes physically and humanly possible for women and men to pursue both affection and achievement without the need for painful bouts of depression.

Ms. Schaff concludes pessimistically that since one third of the women in the country will lose their loved Other in divorce, and many, many more will lose him in widowhood, depression is inevitable. Women must learn the skills to escape it quickly.

I can't disagree with the advice as a short-term response. But we've just got to do better.

I don't think that most men understand that, either. They don't have to.

Catholic Hierarchy
Too Remote from Women

"I'd feel better about them," a friend of mine observed recently apropos to the Roman Catholic hierarchy, "if I thought that more of them had girlfriends." His argument was that the Roman Catholic sexual teaching for married people is proclaimed in this country by a group of men, many of whom have virtually no relationships with women, are ill at ease in the presence of women, are not particularly interested in women and, if the truth be told, don't like women. "In some ways," he went on, "we were a lot better off in the old days when you could assume that a substantial number of bishops had mistresses." (Until sixteenth-century Ireland, one might have added a substantial number had wives and not necessarily just one wife, either.)

Father Joseph Fichter, the Jesuit sociologist, made a similar argument a long time ago when he said that celibacy ought to be optional for priests and marriage compulsory for bishops, because those who pontificate about marriage ought to have at least some feel for what it is like on the inside.

The problem for many of the Catholic hierarchy (I will not estimate a number and certainly not assert that it is a majority) is that neither a wife nor a mistress would particularly interest them. They much prefer the company of cronies, who are also sometimes yes men and sycophants, to the company of women with whom they are awkward and uncomfortable. The same thing, of course, is true of many married men, but such married men are not responsible for preaching sexual ethics or for providing religious leadership for the female half of the human race.

A good number of bishops do have close women friends, though some of the women are more surrogate mothers than anything else, and I suppose occasionally one can even find a bishop who has a lover, though in this day and age they are few and far between.

The fact remains that the Roman Catholic Church is governed to a very considerable extent by men who, if they were not priests, probably would have married, but who would not have particularly enjoyed either their wives or their marriages. This is not, by the way, true of the lower clergy, not if one can believe the research evidence that shows them as able to enter intimate relationships as typical American males (which does not necessarily mean, incidentally, that they are all that skillful at intimacy). Somehow, those who get promoted in the church tend (and I emphasize the word "tend") to be disproportionately selected from those whose needs for intimacy with members of either sex are very low indeed.

Ordinarily, this might not be a very serious problem, but in the present condition of the Catholic Church it is precisely these men who have no desire for either physical or psychological relationships with women who are transmitting the church's teachings about marital sexuality to men and women who do have physical and psychological needs and desires for one another and who are excluding from the ministry of the church the female half of the human race (whose presence in the ministry many of these men would find psychologically intolerable).

Since the whole issue is delicate, let me emphasize once again that I am not speaking of the entire Catholic hierarchy or even necessarily a majority of it, but merely of a substantial component. There are many bishops who delight in women, which I take to be the natural, healthy and normal reaction. Unfortunately, a significant component simply can't stand them, either physically or psychologically.

Maybe we were, after all, better off in the good old days when all the curial cardinals had mistresses.

God as Woman— An Idea Whose Time Has Come

A guy named McDonnell who writes reviews for some Catholic papers has recently dismissed the idea that God is womanly as well as manly as "trendiness." A crotchety fellow, McDonnell doesn't bother to define what he means, though one has the impression that he means that the womanliness of God is a fad.

If by "trendy," however, he meant an idea whose time has come, I would be inclined to agree with him. The image—or to use theologian John Shea's word, "story"—of God as woman has been lurking around in the Christian preconscious for a long time. The perspective we have on sexuality from the insights of the women's movement has brought that image into the conscious dimension of our personalities.

It is only falsely trendy if a) the image is not part of our collective preconscious and b) the women's movement is merely a passing fad.

If Mr. McDonnell thinks that the former is true, he knows no history, and if he thinks the latter is true, he misunderstands the depths of the feminist shift in our culture.

I was first made aware of the womanly aspect of God when I did a study of the sociological functions of devotion to Mary in the Catholic tradition and discovered that Mary's symbolic ("narrative") role is to reflect the tenderness, the gentleness, the affection of God.

Then I saw the dazzling movie *All That Jazz* and realized that director Bob Fosse was raising the question of whether that which is encountered at death is not rather like a passionately gentle woman and whether in fact that womanlike love may not be God.

Then in sociological research my colleagues and I discovered that one fourth of Catholic young adults under thirty imagine God at least some of the time as mother and that those young men who have such an image are more likely to pray often, more likely to see God as a lover, more likely to be involved in social action and more likely to be happily married than those who do not (two or three times more likely in each case).

When I turned to storytelling, I chose—more or less preconsciously, I suppose—to describe the pilgrimage of my heroes toward God as a process of "feminization" in which they learn tenderness and openness as the result of the influence of a woman who is a sacrament of God's womanly love for them.

Since some folks missed this point in my first book (I won't mention its name), I made it quite explicit in the second (though some reviewers still missed it).

In the third volume (Oh, yes, Virginia, there will be another), the theme will be hit even more strongly.

I have been intrigued that practically no one objects. On the various talk shows in which I atone for my sins and diminish my time in purgatory, there is almost immediate acceptance of the womanliness-of-God image once I explain that in God the qualities we attribute to men and to women are combined in what Cardinal Nicholas of Cusa long ago described as the *coincidentia oppositorum,* the coming together of opposites. Thus one can image God as masculine, God as feminine and God as masculine/feminine (or feminine/masculine) with perfect theological justification.

And, as it turns out from the sociological research, great spiritual utility.

As a matter of fact, Mr. McDonnell is the only one who has ever objected.

Jesus could describe himself as a mother with children at

the breast in St. John's Gospel with perfect ease, even though later generations did their best to miss the imagery. So the story is anything but a new fashion.

I speculate that the "story" has been active among the laity for a long time. Surely our young adults have not been influenced by feminist theologians. Nor was Bob Fosse, who probably has never read a theology book. As someone once put it, storytellers are a quarter-century ahead of theologians.

And one might add that many of the people are twenty-five years ahead of the storytellers.

Where do young men and women obtain the image of God as woman? From their mothers, according to our data, and their wives if they are married men. Wives and mothers do not consciously or explicitly pass on the story (though some may be doing so now). Rather, they spread the story of God's womanly love by their own behavior as sacraments, by the revelatory power of their own passion that tells the story of God's passion for us.

Like the heroines in my novels, he said, gleefully making a point.

A Theory That Should Prevail

The pope's general audience talks have turned in recent weeks to the equality of men and women. The pope presents himself as an absolute feminist (though he does not use the word). Domination has no place in the relationships between the sexes. Oppression of women by men is lust, violating as it does the "gift" dimension of the "nuptial meaning" of the body. Furthermore, the present condition of oppression is the fault of men since they are the ones who have the special responsibility for maintaining the delicate balance of giftedness in the sexual relationship.

The pope's critique of sexual domination is profound and

radical. One may easily fault him on the gap between theory and practice in the church. Men continue to dominate women in church institutions; many would think that the refusal to ordain women is a manifestation of such dominance (though the pope explicitly rejects domination as the reason for non-ordination, many would not accept such an explanation). However, it would be a mistake to dismiss the new papal teaching, a dramatic break with tradition, as useless because it has not been implemented in the institutional life of the church and because the pope may not grasp all the implications of what he has said (I rather think he does, but that is for the moment beside the point).

It takes a long time for theory to be converted into practice. Nevertheless theory wins, at least in part, over the long haul. The papal teaching on sexual equality is enormously important and deserves to be taken at face value, however large the lag between theory and practice.

Many feminists will not like the pope's vision. They will accept his critique of the abuse of male power. They will not want to listen to his far more radical vision of a sexual relationship without power. John Paul excludes dominance from sexual relationships. Period. Men may not dominate women. Women may not dominate men (as happens in many marriages, whatever the law may say about the superior power of men). Sex is a gift, not power. When it turns to power of any sort it becomes lust.

The proper response, then, to the male abuse of power in sexual politics is not a movement to build up the power of women so they may dominate men to even the score. The proper response is the elimination of political concern in a relationship that by its very bodily determined giftedness excludes power. A gift is to be cherished, not dominated. Men and women ought to cherish one another, not seek to possess one another as creatures with lesser power.

The vision of John Paul may be written off as utopian. It is in fact merely Christian. The revolution he seeks may take a long time in coming, since sex has been the domain of power politics for millennia. However, a lesser revolution, one which merely seeks to change the proportions of the power pie, is bound to fail. A feminism that accepts the patriarchal society's definition of all human relationships as power relationships is inevitably self-defeating; it begins by conceding its enemy's assumptions. The pope, in this respect, is echoing a dissident feminist action that urges that in a woman's world the exercise of power is replaced by the exercise of caring affection.

John Paul contends that it is built into the nature of the human body to cherish the gift that is the opposite sex. We can violate that aspect of our nature and dominate rather than cherish, possess rather than care for. But we do so at the risk of so impairing our sexual relationships as to almost destroy them.

Implicit in the pope's vision is the notion that a man will cherish as a gift not only the woman who is his spouse but all women, since they are all by their very existence a gift to enrich men's lives and the world in which we live. And of course the opposite is true for women cherishing men.

On occasion, all of us of both sexes glimpse the same vision. In our more cynical moments we say it is an impossible dream. One good reason for having a pope is that it is his job to dream the impossible dream for the rest of us.

Women-hating Films

There's a group (that, mind you, doesn't approve of censorship) attacking the recent outburst of movies in which women get sliced up in various unappealing ways. They argue that such films are degrading and insulting and that they encourage potential rapers, slashers and murderers to go out and imitate what they see on the screen. The prime target for their attack is *Dressed to Kill*, which, they insist, is especially invidious because it is a transvestite who is doing the slashing.

I think they have the wrong target. *Dressed to Kill* shows the cruel vulnerability of women but hardly enjoys it or asks the viewer to enjoy it. Furthermore, I doubt that the killing of Angie Dickinson (who is clearly very much alive) is going to encourage anyone in real life to go after attractive middle-aged blondes

—not anyone who is not already of a mind to do so. The principle advanced by the women's group would lead to the banning of all violence and all sex in all films.

Yet I wonder if the group's members are not, perhaps without quite realizing it, touching on an important aspect of contemporary American culture. Can it be possible that there is a subtle connection between the suppressed antipathy stirred up by the feminist movement and such films as *Halloween, Friday the Thirteenth, The Fog, When a Stranger Calls, Prom Night, Motel Hell* and *He Knows You're Alone?* In each of them various attractive young women are done in by singularly gruesome methods without any pretense to the artistic skill of *Dressed to Kill.* In some of them men are similarly dispatched too, yet the camera seems to take special delight in the ravishing and liquidation of the young women.

The old Dracula films used to dispose of such unfortunates in pretty grisly fashion, too. Our propensity to enjoy the destruction of helpless female victims is not new. I suppose you can explain most of the recent excesses as part of a general excess of violence in exploitation films and books without having to invoke women's lib as a factor. And yet . . .

On the average, women are the more vulnerable of the sexes. Such vulnerability and its defense are the raw material of many classic suspense stories—and much real life drama too. Men and women alike enjoy the stories of the rescue of the cornered, terrified and yet plucky captive. It is but a short step in the tricky human subconsciousness to enjoy fantasies of the captive being tormented and destroyed.

Especially if you don't like them and especially if you see their greater vulnerability as an assault, a demand, an affront, an intolerable difference, a terrifying threat.

If men hate women, and many men do (and vice versa), it is precisely in this that their hatred consists: The apparent softness and vulnerability of women is a demand, a threat, a challenge, a terror. Given half a chance, the hatred says, that other being with her wiles, her appeal, her fears and her implacable hunger will absorb, consume and destroy you. That's why there were witch-hunts in the decline of the Middle Ages (a lot of other factors were at work, but the raw primal fear of Woman was part of it).

Doubtless, for those men who fear and hate women, the militancy of some of them comes as a special threat. They want to have their cake and eat it too, to enjoy the special privileges of being women and the special rights of being men. If they can get away with that we can't exploit them anymore and if we can't exploit them how are we to protect ourselves from them?

Is such a dehumanizing fear/hatred/exploitation syndrome still widespread in the male consciousness? Who are you trying to kid?

So do some men enjoy making movies in which these soft threatening creatures are brutalized? And do other men enjoy watching such movies? Are such films likely to be especially appealing in times of heightened conflict between the sexes?

Ha.

One need not postulate a conspiracy or even think that one is witnessing a dramatic change. The "slice-up-the-girls" movies reveal a very dark corner of the fouled-up sexual relationships in our society. The two fifths of federal government women employees who report sexual harassment reveal another dark corner.

No, I take that back. The same dark corner. Harassment is fear/hatred/exploitation, too.

Biological Mystery

In this day of liberation should a man hold a door open for a woman?

You lose, regardless—especially if you're dealing with Irish-American women, because by definition you lose with them. Regardless.

1) Of course you hold the door open for me, you big ape; didn't your mother teach you any manners?

2) Don't you dare hold the door for me. I'm a liberated woman and I don't put up with such male chauvinism.

3) How dare you not open the door for me! I'm a liberated woman and I don't put up with such male chauvinism.

The last is called having your cake and eating it too. Nowhere is it written, however, that a woman can't do that, especially if she is Irish.

Regardless.

I hold the door open (I'd even take off my hat in elevators, except I don't wear a hat). I was raised to do so, and besides there is little enough elegance left in the world. Equality if it is to be achieved at all will not be achieved by returning to savagery.

One of my friends asked me why I did it—mind you she fully expected me to continue to do so.

Being contentious (another ethnic-group trait, if truth be told), I said that I did so out of respect for a bearer of life.

She was highly incensed. She'd done a lot of other things which were more deserving of respect than having children. (I quote from my memory and doubtless inaccurately. You never quote an Irish mother accurately. By definition.)

I agreed, but insisted on the validity of the historical point. The custom of holding the door for members of the allegedly fair sex dates to the era when it could be taken for granted that she would have a child in her arms and not be able to open the door.

And there is the heart of the matter. Freud was wrong when he said that anatomy is destiny. But so are the feminists wrong when they say anatomy has nothing to do with destiny.

Similarly, history has something to do with destiny too, especially cultural patterns that have deep historical origins. The challenge is not to eliminate the impacts of history and biology, but to reintegrate them with personal freedom in a new era when the biological constraints are different. Not so long ago a woman was likely to be either pregnant or carrying a small child when she approached the hypothetical door because the death rates, infant and adult, were so high that the race continued only by persisting in something near maximum fertility. You might not have any fondness left for a particular bearer of life. You still took good care of her because she was the source of life which would keep your clan and your family going and provide children to take care of you in your old age, should you be part of the minority that lived to old age. Your respect for her was purely pragmatic.

Now the situation is exactly the opposite: Fertility must be controlled lest there be so much human life that the planet becomes uninhabitable. Much of the hatred for children that stirs around just beneath the threshold of consciousness these days results from the fact that some people like to think of children not as a guarantee of the continuation of life but a threat to it.

When there's too much life (or seems to be too much life) instead of not enough, it is easy to become contemptuous of life. Thus the leadership of the Catholic Church is correct when it insists on the need to revere and respect life, especially when, in their more enlightened moments, the leaders also emphasize the necessity of responsible family planning. Unfortunately the pope and the bishops have not thought through these two principles deeply enough so that they don't sound like they are talking out of both sides of their mouths.

Yet it finally seems to me that even in a time when we no longer need high levels of fertility for survival, it is still possible and necessary to respect the mystery of life and the persons who in a special way continue that mystery, a marvel as amazing and wonderful when it produces but two children as when it produces ten.

To be the possessor of that mysterious power is indeed a biological given and not a matter of merit or virtue. There are, as my friend said, other and more important reasons for respecting a human person. Yet those other reasons, which may well be meritorious and virtuous, do not negate the biological mystery or make it less deserving of awe and wonder.

Savoring the
Superiority of Women

Women, of course, are superior to men. Equal, indeed, and entitled to full equality under the law, but in addition to equal, superior.

I cite as evidence in favor of this prejudice a poem by Helena Minton, called "Bread." Ms. Minton describes the joy of baking bread and then setting it on the table "beside the knife" and understanding the enormous power that cooks have over other human beings—"the pleasure / of saying EAT."

Note both the imagery and the insight of these simple lines. The brown bread is placed on the table, "beside the knife," and the cook savors—one can almost imagine her licking her lips—the joy of putting the warm savory bread on the table with a flourish and saying with a full sense of power, "Eat."

Or—since by Ms. Minton's admission in one of her own poems, her origins are Irish—she might even put it in the English translation of the Gaelic subjunctive: "Eat, letye."

(The difference between Irish women and women of certain other ethnic groups is that Irish women don't bother to keep the fact of their superiority over men secret.)

I will not indulge in biological determinism and say the images and the insight of Helena Minton's "Bread" would have been impossible for a man. I simply contend that it would be highly unlikely that a man would produce the same kind of poetic lines. I will leave aside the question of whether an intense sensitivity to color, texture and detail is a physical or a cultural propensity of women—probably it is a combination of both. I will content myself with the observation that this womanly propensity for concrete vividness gives them tremendous advantages over men when it comes to writing poetry and stories. As a novelist I don't want to have to compete with the likes of Mary

Gordon and as a poet I don't want to have to compete with the likes of Helena Minton. In both crafts, they are better than I; not only better than I am now but better than I could ever hope to be at precisely those skills that are indispensable for practicing these two different crafts.

Obviously there are male writers who have something of the same skills, and women writers who lack them completely. Yet, on the average, I would wager, anyone who reads an anonymous passage filled with rich and intricate details and judges that the passage was written by a woman will be right four times out of five, if not nine times out of ten.

In any proper feminist movement, then, the goal ought not to be to win for women the right to produce poetry and stories that are devoid of such wit and color, but rather to provide for men the opportunity to develop their own skills of observation and sensitivity so that they can begin to catch up with women in such "communality" with the world around.

I don't think that we will ever catch up, but I'll begin to believe that we are approaching a situation of healthy equality between the sexes when men have come to accept the fact that this kind of catching up with womanly sensitivity is worth doing.

Strong Women Back in Fashion

Strong women are back in fashion. The same week that there is a bathing beauty contest for muscular women, *Time* magazine has a cover article on the "New Ideal of Beauty," which apparently is kind of Jane Fondaish—lean, hard and tough.

This gives *Time* a chance to strike back at *Newsweek* with a cover woman who is as appealing, if differently so, as the latter's half-clothed artist's model of a month or two ago.

More to the point, however, *Time* has captured a trend in American society that goes beyond Ms. Fonda, who has the remarkable ability to turn into caricature every cause she endorses —mostly because she seems to think that she's the first to have discovered it.

In fact, the human body, masculine and feminine, was designed to be strong. For most of the history of the species, women had to be physically strong to survive. The fluffy weakling Ms. Fonda thinks typifies "unliberated" women (i.e., most women before her) is a phenomenon limited to recent times and to certain social classes, most notably the upper middle class, of which Ms. Fonda is a product.

Some of the most beautiful women in the world, if we are to judge by their pictures, are the !Kung, members of a so-called primitive tribe in the Kalahari region of Africa. The tribe are gatherers and hunters who live, it is supposed, much like our most ancient ancestors.

Their women are solidly put together (well into their mature years) because gathering food is vigorous exercise, the kind of exercise for which the human body is apparently designed.

The !Kung women, incidentally, are neither oppressed nor overworked, though in fact they work harder than their menfolk, who are hunters. No one in the tribe, however, works anything like a forty-hour week. They are dismayed to learn that others must work that long to stay alive.

We would not want to live like the !Kung. And our taming of the resources of nature enables us to have a richer and fuller life. Nonetheless, once we have left behind hunting and gathering and farming for more sophisticated cultural patterns, we leave behind also activities which guarantee that the body stay in condition.

What is natural for the !Kung becomes optional for us. They don't need exercise programs—or didn't until civilization came along. We do.

Moreover, civilization, especially its medical progress, gives us longer lives (between two and three times as long on the average). At an age when a person in a hunting and gathering culture was one of the wise elders of the tribe and no longer required to chase antelopes or pick roots and berries with a baby on the hip, we are still in the prime of life. Hence our bodies are in even greater need of exercise and more resistant to it.

Thus, shorn of its ideological rubbish, the quest of many contemporary women for physical fitness and strength is in fact a return to the past, to the kind of vigorous and demanding bodily movements that many of their grandmothers and great-grandmothers in the peasant cultures of Europe (to say nothing of their more remote ancestors in the gathering cultures) would have taken for granted.

I for one say it's fine. A trim and attractive Ms. Fonda is marginally more tolerable than a soft and flabby Ms. Fonda.

But I come from an ethnic culture that has always valued strong women. The dilemma of the Irish male is that he admires enormously women who are psychologically and physically strong—but has no idea of how to relate to them. If she turns to weight lifting, it makes her even more attractive and more terrifying—and God knows more dangerous.

But some caveats are in order. A strong, solid body is a "good"; it is not, however, the only good, or a good that will transform your life, or a good that ought to mean the same thing to everyone.

The problem with the ideological fitness buffs is that they make their option an obligation for everyone, their perceived good as an all-important good, their source of human renewal the only acceptable source of renewal.

Lean, hard bodies may be attractive, though not for everyone—either as the attractor or the attractee. There is room for variety and pluralism. Not everyone needs to look like a muscular borderline anorexia case. You are not a traitor to your manhood or your womanhood if, like the late Robert Hutchins, you lie down every time you are tempted to exercise and wait for the temptation to pass.

And while I try to swim every day, I buy my raspberries and blueberries already picked—though if the womenfolk want to pick them, that's all right with me. Safer that, say I, than their lifting weights.

Safer for me.

Fluidity at Women's Roles Causes Problems

Often I wonder who makes the rules. Who has legislated that there is only one way that is appropriate for humans to behave? Jesus of Nazareth announced that in his father's kingdom there were many houses and that if it were not so, he would not have told it. But an awful lot of people have taken it upon themselves to go around and insist that there is only one house and that's the one they live in.

I listened recently to a group of women in their late thirties and early forties who were superb mothers. They had done an absolutely splendid job of raising their children. To a person they insisted vigorously that their job was so exhausting and so demanding that they couldn't possibly do anything else during their child-rearing years and that, moreover, no one else could either. If a woman had a career, they agreed unanimously, she couldn't possibly also be a good mother.

What I want to know is who says so?

On another occasion I was with a group of women somewhat younger, all of whom had careers, and some of whom also had families. They insisted just as vigorously that unless a woman had a place in the occupational world, she didn't amount to anything at all. You only carve out for yourself an identity when you have a meaningful, professional career. Any other role is an acceptance of women's traditional second-class status. Liberated women work, unliberated women don't.

Again I say, who says so?

Could it not be that some liberated women work and some don't? Could it not be that not having to work is a marvelous form of liberation for some people? Could it not be that some women should only be wives and mothers during the child-rearing years and that others should have both careers and families, and that still others should only have careers? Who says that everybody has to make one choice, and one choice only, to gain social approval?

I know what both groups of women were doing, of course. They were defending themselves from their critics, protecting their decisions from the attacks of those who say they made the wrong decisions. But why is that necessary? Why is there not room in society for a multitude of decisions? Why is there only one way to be a wife, one way to be a mother, one way to be a liberated woman, one way to be a good priest, one way to raise your children, one way to pursue your education, one lifestyle to choose, one system of values by which to live?

Why can we not be more tentative and merely say, this seems to work for me but that doesn't mean it will work for you, and I'm not going to try to prove that your choice is wrong.

I realize some people articulate such a position, but it's usually pretty clear that they don't really mean it; that they think their way is not only the best way for them but is the best way for everyone.

The Holy Spirit, if we're to believe theologians these days, is the spirit of variety and diversity, a kind of divine Tinkerbell who flits about space calling forth the most unique and most special—another version of the kingdom with many mansions. Humankind has never been very good at responding to such playful and madcap diversity.

In these times women seem to be the particular victims of our passion for uniformity, both in that the rules are most rigidly imposed on them and that they are most likely to want to impose the rules most rigidly on other women. The reason, I suppose, is that the social roles of women are becoming much more fluid than they used to be.

Or, as I prefer to put it, women now have much more freedom to choose than they used to have. Why can't we all cheer loudly for that freedom?

Beauty over Forty

Some feminists are furious at *Harper's Bazaar* for publishing a list of beautiful women over forty, complete with glamorous pictures. Such women as Elizabeth Taylor, Sophia Loren, Audrey Hepburn, Natalie Wood, Susannah York and Jill St. John, they argue, do not deserve the honor because the only standard being used is physical beauty. In a properly feminist age, women ought to win a place on such lists because of their intellectual, emotional and personal beauty and not merely their physical attractiveness.

The *Bazaar* list, they contend, is nothing more than a middle-aged version of the Miss America spectacle in Atlantic City.

After all, physical beauty is a matter of luck. No one should be rewarded for being lucky.

Apparently intelligence, college education, professional success and the other qualities celebrated by the feminist critics of the list are not matters of luck. Don't love me for my body, because that is merely a matter of genes, love me for my intelligence, which I have earned and developed all by myself.

In fact, both raw intelligence and raw physical attractiveness are mostly inherited; and after the early years, physical attractiveness probably takes as much effort to preserve (for men and women) as does intellectual ability. I don't doubt that intellectual and spiritual powers are more noble than physical beauty. But those who pretend that physical beauty is not important or is somehow not appropriate have confused humans with angels.

I'm not prepared to defend the list in *Harper's Bazaar*. I know many women over forty who dazzle me a lot more than Ms. Taylor or Ms. York (I'll celebrate Ms. Loren any day, however). Yet complaining about the attention beautiful women of any age receive sounds dangerously like envy. Maybe it isn't fair that some of us are more attractive than others, but that's the way it is and griping about it reminds me of eighth-grade girls being mean to the prettiest girl in the class merely because she is pretty.

About the same time as the controversy over the "plus-forty" list started, the New York *Times* science section expressed "surprise" at the deep effects of physical beauty as revealed in research done at the University of Minnesota. The good, gray *Times* rarely admits to being surprised over anything. However, the fact that a person's physical attractiveness can have lasting effects on personality, social life and educational and career opportunities, as reported in the *Times,* was apparently an unpleasant and unwanted surprise. It is simply not fair that you should do better in life because you are beautiful.

The research of the Minnesota team is ingenious and important. If it confirms what ought to have been obvious, there is still much to be said for confirming the obvious, especially when the obvious, as the director of research observed, makes so many people uncomfortable. Yet a strong positive reaction to physical beauty is programmed into our bodies and deeply ingrained into our personalities. We can and should take this into account when we make our judgments (about such things as academic grades) but we cannot eliminate it from our lives or from the human condition, as seems to be suggested by articles on similar research reported in popular social science journals.

The beautiful have an advantage and that is that. Only the envious want to take their beauty away from them to even the odds. Of course, there are lots of envious humans.

There are also disadvantages that ought to be taken into account. The director of the Minnesota project suggested that since she was less attractive than her sister, she was the one who was chosen for college. Beautiful women are more likely to be harassed by men and hated by women. The life stories of the *Bazaar* plus-forty list are not all happy ones. Some women find beauty such a burden that they eliminate it from their lives by the time they are twenty-five, usually by becoming permanently overweight.

Nothing is ever fair, but what is particularly unfair (as far as you are concerned) depends mostly on where you happen to be. Usually not in someone else's yard, which always seems greener—at least to the green eyes of your envy.

We are members of a hunter-gatherer species that were programmed mostly to be dead before we were forty. By our ingenuity we have doubled the course of our lives and enabled men and women who want to be physically attractive to remain so for most, if not all, of their lives. Some folks begin with an advantage, but hard work, discipline, self-esteem and especially love (both given and received) smooth out the odds.

Judgments should be made not on what other people have but what we do with what we have. That is wisdom, however, which envy instantly rejects.

Living with Sexual Harassment

Ms. Phyllis Schlafly has recently informed the world that virtuous women are not subject to sexual harassment. If there is sexual harassment in the occupational world, Ms. Schlafly insisted, the reason is that non-virtuous women by their "body language" invite harassment.

And the pope is Lutheran and chickens have lips and the Reverend Jerry Falwell is a Jesuit and Ronald Reagan is secretly a member of the Communist party.

Let us concede to Ms. Schlafly as much as one can: Some women do indeed invite sexual harassment and are not particularly displeased by it, not if they are being harassed by the right person. Moreover, because communication between the sexes is flawed and obscure, some men may see in the behavior of some women invitations that are not in fact intended.

It is often hard to determine when reasonably good-natured kidding or flattery ends and harassment begins. What one man may intend as a compliment, or at least the beginning of a discussion, will on the lips of another be harassment, and what may please one woman will insult another.

On the boundary lines, then, it may be difficult to determine what is harassment and what is not. But much of the behavior reported by women in various surveys is nowhere near the boundary line. A wolf whistle may not be harassment; constant pawing is, and the latter, according to surveys, is by no means the worst sexual attention a woman may expect in the work place.

The problem, not to put too fine an edge on things, is that a very substantial proportion of the male population has not matured sexually beyond the age of a fifteen-year-old. A woman is primarily an object, a thing to be used, an opportunity to "score." Such men may marry and sire children and go through the motions of being a dutiful husband and father. They may have affection and even respect for their wives and daughters, but any other woman is fair game. That's the way men are reared in American society, and unless we change the male socialization process drastically, we will continue to have a large number of men for whom the "score" is a primary consideration when any likely sexual target appears.

Not all men are rapists, as the flaky feminist author contended. But there is some survey evidence to indicate that a substantial minority of men would engage in occasional rape if they were sure they could get away with it. The veneer of civilization that protects women is very thin. It does not take much to peel away the veneer—a point that those feminists who are so eager to destroy our social structure might want to ponder.

In addition to actual or potential rapists, there are many other men who cannot distinguish between the women who inhabit their fantasies and the women they encounter in the real world. Even if they are too civilized or too frightened or too restrained to be perpetually preoccupied with the possibility of a "score," they're incapable of thinking of harassment as anything more than good clean fun, wholesome locker-room entertainment.

Not all men are that way, of course, though I won't attempt to estimate the proportion who are. Doubtless there is a propensity in the human condition, probably biologically based, for men to be the overt sexual aggressors in the process of the continuation of the species. That propensity becomes a social and human problem only when it precludes the possibility of a man seriously considering that a woman is a person like unto himself and entering into a relationship of equality and friendship with that person. The history of human sexuality does not give us much reason to hope that men are capable of such relationships.

As more women move into the occupational world there is going to be more sexual harassment; particularly, it seems to me, if they are willing to accept the feminist ideology which says that in that world women should act like men. Presumably this means that the sexual exploitation that goes on in the "man's" world should be available to women too.

It might be much better, however, if the "feminization" of the work world would have as one of its goals the elimination of exploitation in the occupational environment. If ever such a goal is achieved, then the world of work would be as safe for all women as it is for Ms. Schlafly's virtuous damsels—some of whom one suspects might not object to being harassed if they could find a way to persuade someone to harass them.

The End of the Maternal Instinct?

There is no universal, innate bond between mother and child, according to a recently published translation of a French book. The volume is being hailed as a powerful feminist tract because it liberates women from feeling that they are physiologically tied to child care. As the author of the book breathlessly babbled to an American feminist journalist, now men will be free to enjoy child care, too.

The logic of the argument may escape most people. There may or may not be a "maternal instinct" in humans, but the real barrier to a unisex philosophy is not maternal instinct but maternity. The problem with treating both sexes as though they are virtually the same is not that women might feel a powerful bond to the children they bear, but rather that they bear children.

Some radical feminists rail against this division of labor and even speak of the need to develop artificial wombs so that women will enjoy total equality with men. It then would be possible for women to walk away from their offspring as easily and as early as men do.

The problem with this solution is that you would still need some kind of surgery to remove the fetus so you could place it in an artificial womb. Women would still be at a disadvantage.

Most women (and even some feminists) don't think that bearing children is a disadvantage, but the radicals would dismiss that as false consciousness.

So the "maternal bond" or "maternal instinct" issue is, to a considerable extent, irrelevant to questions of feminism. Even if you can abolish the maternal instinct, the problems of sexual diversity remain.

Nonetheless, it is an interesting scientific problem. Unfortunately, the French book, interesting as history and psychology, demolishes only a straw person in its argumentation. It is surely the case that some women hate their children. It is also beyond question that in some cultures, including the past of our own culture, mother love did seem very powerful. And it is beyond question that many women experience strong ambivalence toward their children.

They would, for example, enjoy strangling the little monsters several times a day.

If a bond between mother and child can be properly called a bond only when all mothers everywhere feel a powerful positive attraction to their children, then obviously there is no such bond. We hardly need learned works of Gallic scholarship to establish the point.

But the fact remains that most mothers, much of the time and in the majority of human cultures, do feel powerful stirrings of love for their children and attribute these stirrings to the fact that the child is *their* child.

If you try to tell such mothers that there is no physical bond of attraction between them and their children, they are very likely to tell you that you don't know what you're talking about.

The mistake is to assume a perfect parallel between maternal bonds in other species and the human mother-child bonding; we humans do not relate to our children or our spouses the way, let us say, the Gambel's quails outside my Arizona window do. No serious student of human bonding has ever claimed such a parallel. Edward Wilson, the most notorious of the sociobiologists—and a whipping person for radical feminists—claims at the most no more than a 25 percent determination of human behavior by biological mechanisms.

Thus, the maximum claim would be that there is a propensity in human nature for a mother to feel a strong attraction for her child based on the biology of mother and child, though this propensity can be overridden by culture, personality or free choice.

I don't think this position has necessarily been proven scientifically, though it seems to have some inherent plausibility. But those who deny the existence of the maternal bond must respond to this position and not to a straw person they've created (and which, in some of their more polemical moments, the sociobiologists seem to be endorsing).

If there is indeed no biologically rooted inclination for a mother to dote on her offspring (while cheerfully acknowledging that the child can on occasion act like a little monster), then the problem remains of where the inclination arises. Radical feminists would doubtless assert that it is purely a creation of patriarchal culture and the proper education will make it disappear. Family love, then, they say, will be given in utter freedom instead of freely building on genetically programmed urges.

Wanna bet?

In Memoriam:
Grace Kelly

I don't want to write a column about Grace Kelly. I turned off
the TV whenever there were excerpts from her films after her
death. I refused to read the articles in the papers and national
magazines. I want to avoid seeing any of her pictures—and especially *Rear Window*—for years.

I reacted the same way only once before in my life—when
John Kennedy was killed. It took years before I could pick up
books about the Kennedy administration and not put them
down.

I admit that this is irrational behavior. But when key symbols of your life are destroyed, you ought not to be expected to
react rationally.

Yet my friend and colleague David Tracy insists, quite correctly, that I must write about her because she meant something
special to our generation of Irish Catholics. She was a symbol as
John Kennedy was, a symbol of a decisive turning point in Irish
Catholic history in this country.

The symbol is not the same as the person. Ms. Kelly (or Ms.
Grimaldi, if you wish) was a real person, a wife, a mother, an
actress. Her death is a tragedy to those who knew and loved her.
They have my sympathy as would any group who lost a wife
and a mother and a friend too young in life.

It is not about the person Grace Kelly that I must write. She
herself apparently was uneasy with her symbolic role, though
she objected more to the fairy-tale princess casting than to any
other—and quite properly so it would seem to me.

What might be the overlap between the real person and the
symbol is not for me to say, though surely there must be some.
John Kennedy turned out to be substantially less than the sym-

bol we made him, but there was still something of the symbol in the real man.

Grace Kelly's "sexual elegance" recognized by that ingenious if ultimately Jansenist Catholic filmmaker Alfred Hitchcock was extremely important to young men—and I think young women too—who matured as Irish and Catholic in the early 1950s.

We were told by our church leaders (though not by our heritage) that you could not be Irish and Catholic on the one hand and sexual on the other.

And we were told by a couple of centuries of English oppression that you could not be Irish and Catholic on the one hand and elegant on the other.

And Ms. Kelly, fire in the ice, inferno in the snow, represented in symbol that both the church and the English were wrong.

The influence of such a symbol was subtle but powerful, especially since Ms. Kelly appeared on the scene just at the time when we were beginning to break with the rigid Catholic piety which was imposed on us after the Great Famine in the middle of the last century.

And we were also breaking away from the immigrant ghetto and becoming successful suburban professionals and/or university academics.

John Kennedy said we could no longer be excluded from the presidency.

And Grace Kelly said we could no longer be considered either unchic or asexual.

With a vengeance.

Only the few of us who knew the legends out of the deep past of our heritage knew how much of Finn McCool was in Jack Kennedy.

(A lot, it turned out, including the obsession with women.)

Nor did we understand explicitly how much Grace Kelly was in the line of coolly erotic Irish heroines like Etain, Deirdre, Grainne and Maeve.

She even looked like their portraits and the descriptions of the heroines in the sagas seemed to have her in mind.

She touched images in the Irish collective preconscious that had been latent for a long time and were now trying to find expression again.

We would not be Irish if we did not wonder what might have happened if her film career had been longer. I guess some of us of that age (and I am her age almost exactly) were disappointed that she married a "foreigner"—but she had her own life to live and you can't give up your life to images in other people's preconscious.

Grace Kelly represented princess fantasies out of our past before she married the lord of a minor historical anomaly. For us the fairy tale ended with marriage rather than began.

Would we have climbed out of asexuality and inelegance without her?

Sure. Symbols reflect historical and social processes instead of creating them—most of the time, anyway.

But they also facilitate the processes.

And we were lucky to have her presence in our era. She represented both where we came from and where we are going.

A person does not achieve happiness by being a symbol. Yet it is no small thing to be an important symbol for large numbers of your fellows at a crucial time in their story.

And Grace Kelly did that.

Oh, brother, did she!

POLITICS

The conservatives who publish the troglodyte Catholic paper
The Wanderer *will tell you I am a dangerous radical, one of the
two crucial problems which the new Archbishop of Chicago
faces (the other being Communion [under both species] on Sunday).*

And the former "liberal" editor of the trendy National Catholic Reporter *says that he bought a book of mine at a second-
hand sale and threw it in the garbage can after he read it.*

*So I can't be all bad if I so offend the ideologues of both
sides.*

Am I a liberal or a conservative?

*I'm an Irish Catholic Democrat from Chicago. I believe that
politics is about putting together winning coalitions rather than
about the ideological purity of "moral" victories.*

*Which means I am opposed to everything which has hap-
pened to the Democratic party since the advent of the disastrous
McGovern reforms.*

I want to win elections, not lose them.

*And as the late Mayor—the only Mayor—said of Hubert
Humphrey's unfortunate defeat in 1968, he lost because he
didn't have the votes.*

And losing, moral victory or not, isn't anything.

*And I don't think that a single voter has ever been swayed
by a resolution passed at a meeting of professional religious
functionaries.*

*When priests were the sons of cops and precinct captains
they knew that.*

*And as someone has said, Nixon, Ford, Carter and Reagan
are a Mount Rushmore of incompetency.*

*So let's bring back the corrupt political bosses who gave the
Democratic party FDR, Adlai Stevenson, John Kennedy and
Hubert Humphrey . . . And win again.*

Crime as Political Protest

The nation is obsessed with crime. And with very good reason. Both *Time* and *Newsweek* recently produced cover stories on the crime epidemic. My home city of Tucson has achieved national prominence because it is under assault from a small army of at least seven hundred burglars. Eight out of a hundred Arizona residents (including me) will be crime victims this year. Chicago's Mayor Jane Byrne is moving into a crime-infested public housing area. Suburban crime is also increasing dramatically. Home security gadgets are selling as if there were going to be a shortage of them. More and more Americans are taking lessons in the use of firearms to protect themselves. Public confidence in the ability of law enforcement agencies to protect them from crime is at rock bottom.

One hears all sorts of explanations for the crime epidemic. Yet no one seems to consider the possibility that in part the crime problem is one more holdover from the disastrous 1960s. During that era many professors, journalists and liberal politicians like George McGovern suggested in effect that crime was a political statement. The violence and looting of the urban riots were virtually justified on the grounds that the rioters were the victims of social injustice.

"Ripping off whitey" became a phrase that was not altogether reprehensible. Similarly, praise of the counterculture from some segments of our intelligentsia often implied that "squares" possessed their wealth as a result of political oppression and that "liberating" wealth from them might even be an act of political virtue—revolutionary violence.

Many Americans on the liberal end of the political spectrum did not exactly agree with such rhetoric; neither, however, did they condemn it. They were more interested, it seemed, in understanding the causes of violence and theft than preventing such contempt for law. Police became "pigs," the hated enforcers of middle-class capitalistic oppression.

The implications of such disrespect for the law were not lost on young people. Criminals might be considered political protesters and, in the case of such groups as the Black Panthers, revolutionary heroes. If you liberated middle-class property or ripped off whitey's money, you were no longer a criminal. You were engaging in revolutionary protest.

I don't think that young criminals then or now seriously see themselves as political activists. They steal because it is easier to obtain money by taking it from others than by working. Nevertheless, if there is a climate of public opinion which lends legitimacy to crime, there will be more crime. The soft-headedness of the sixties has not caused the crime explosion of the seventies and eighties. It must, however, be held accountable for some of the size and intensity of the explosion.

Neither the New York City muggers nor the Tucson drug culture robbers consider what they are doing to be morally reprehensible. While they may not kid themselves anymore into thinking they are engaging in revolutionary violence, they do have a rhetoric of justification and excuse that assumes they have as much right to what they steal as do those from whom they steal—a holdover from the moral and intellectual softness of the 1960s. If you throw some of the Ten Commandments out the window, the others will quickly follow. If you tell young people that some laws need not be obeyed, then all law is in jeopardy.

During the 1960s such an observation was written off as reactionary. Vietnam, we were told by not a few college professors, justified contempt for the law. Crime was the result of capitalist oppression.

Nevertheless, then and now, when the property of the professors is ripped off or liberated they call for help from the pigs more loudly than anyone else.

Chickens are not supposed to come home to roost.

Chicago Politics:
The Misunderstandings Remain

There are a number of subjects about which rational discussion has become impossible—inflation, abortion, feminism and the Cook County regular Democratic organization.

I have, on occasion in the past, tried to write about the Organization, not to defend it but to explain how it works. Such objective discussion, however, is almost impossible, as the only kind of discourse permitted in most American intellectual and journalistic circles about the Organization is that which denounces it. Such is the temper of our times—that moral outrage is considered to be superior to objective understanding. Denounce something before you learn how it works.

The distinguished British magazine, *The Economist*, came to Chicago the other week and wrote a pompous and unperceptive article about the city, utterly misunderstanding the nature of its political functioning—though, to tell the truth, *The Economist* was more perceptive than the New York *Times* or CBS News usually is.

The typical, and indeed symbolic, misunderstanding of Chicago politics is the cliché that one hears all over the country that Richard M. Daley was nominated for states attorney in Cook County by beating the Organization that his father headed. This is sheer baloney. You don't carry forty wards in Chicago by beating the Organization. You carry forty wards because many of the ward committeemen implicitly—and an even larger number of the precinct captains explicitly—support you.

The formal endorsement of the mayor and even of the collective body of the ward committeemen, extorted by patronage threats from the mayor, does not and never has guaranteed the support of the Organization on Election Day. One can succeed to the mayor's job and not succeed to control of the Organization. It took State Senator Richard Daley's father two terms in office as mayor and almost ten years as chairman of the Cook County Democratic Committee before he could have been said to be in effective control of the Organization, and even then his control depended on his realization that there were many components of the Organization about which he had to be very careful. These parts of the Organization would "go along" with "da mare" but only so long as he didn't push them too hard.

The Organization is a loosely structured, decentralized, intricate web of relationships of loyalty, obligation, mutual benefit and responsibility. It may have authoritative leadership on the top, though sometimes it hasn't, but much of this leadership's authority rests in its ability to persuade the various subnetworks of relationships to "go along."

I am not, at this point, trying to argue that organization politics is good or bad, corrupt or uncorrupt, efficient or inefficient. Nor am I trying to evaluate the outcome of organization politics as compared to the outcome of reform politics. I am merely asserting that this is the way the Organization is structured and if you don't understand that, you don't understand anything about Chicago politics. Nor am I trying, at this point, to make any judgment on Mayor Jane Byrne's administration and her political skills. I am simply asserting that it is unperceptive to think that after only a year in office Mrs. Byrne could be expected to control the Organization, much less choose a candidate of whom it could be said, simply by the fact of her choice, that he was *the* Organization candidate.

The mistake in the "young Daley beats his father's Organization" model is to assume that because the elder Daley was the boss—and he surely was that—he could force all the pieces and parts of the Organization to do whatever he wanted. Such an assumption suits well the conviction that the late mayor was an all-powerful dictator and is what many people want to believe about Chicago politics.

Too many believe that merely by wielding the patronage stick without any concern for developing a network of loyalty and consensus, the mayor of Chicago can choose whatever candidate he or she wants for public office. If such a conviction makes you feel good, then by all means continue to believe it.

But you will misunderstand the social structure of the nation's second largest city and you may overlook some very important dimensions of urban life in any city. You will also make the same mistake that Jane Byrne made (and which many Catholic churchmen make): Authority finally does not rest on one's ability to give orders, but rather rests on one's ability to generate loyalty and consent.

Bruce Babbitt for President

I propose that the battered and leaderless Democratic party follow the advice of my illustrious namesake Horace Greeley and go West in their search for a presidential candidate in 1984 (Horace meant western New York but that's another matter).

Governor Bruce Babbitt of Arizona has all the requirements for a superb presidential candidate. His only liability is that Arizona is a relatively small state and no one east of the Mississippi pays much attention to it.

No one paid much attention to Georgia before 1976 either, much to our sorrow as it turns out.

Consider Governor Babbitt's assets: He is a Westerner and the Democrats have to recapture their appeal to the Western states whose electoral power is growing rapidly. He is a Catholic, indeed, a class president from the University of Notre Dame, and Democrats must recapture their base among Catholic voters whom they lost in 1980.

He is a liberal Democrat who has been re-elected in Barry Goldwater's usually conservative Republican state—and Democrats must keep alive their liberal tradition, while at the same time respecting the country's conservative suspicion of big government.

He is a young man with an attractive family at a time when the country will be looking for younger leadership and new faces. He is a firm believer in states' rights when the nation is dubious about federal government, yet he also sees the necessity of federal intervention in the solution of some urban problems.

He is profoundly concerned about environmental problems, as are all Americans, yet he has a pragmatic, down-to-earth approach to the solution of environmental problems. He has pulled together a broad coalition in support of water-use reform in Arizona, which is both tough and feasible. No one is completely happy with his program for water use, but most people think it will work and can live with it.

Arizona is a complex state: at least three different geographies, a heterogenous population which is rapidly changing, many opposing and feuding political constituencies. Babbitt is not universally liked but he certainly has wide grass-roots support and is one of the most popular governors in America even though he has asked Arizonans to face some tough decisions. One hears it said repeatedly by political scientists, historians and ordinary citizens that he is the best governor the state has ever had.

A recent article by Babbitt in *The New Republic* magazine gives a sense of the commonsense brilliance of Governor Babbitt (and *The New Republic* publishes articles by politicians only when it is convinced that they have written the article themselves). Called "States Rights for Liberals," the article argues that there are three conditions under which a federal government program should be decentralized to allow state control: when a) there is a history of the states being responsible for the activity, b) much of the money for the program has traditionally come from the states and c) state programs do not result in destructive state competition (as happens in welfare payments).

One should ask, Governor Babbitt insists, whether a "given federal program serves a truly essential national purpose or whether it might be more accurately characterized as a matter that ought to be left for the states and localities to spend their tax money on or not, as they please."

Welfare he sees as a national issue; primary and secondary education, law enforcement and most highway construction as local issues. "The neighborhood school, the town constable, and to a lesser extent road building are venerable local functions with relatively little historic federal involvement. They are also programs that enjoy strong local support and that involve a high degree of local administrative effort not readily handled at the national level."

This commonsense liberalism, deeply rooted in the American past, is, I submit, just what the Democratic party needs. As it searches for new leadership it can ill afford to ignore the governor of Arizona.

Poverty Cannot Be Solved by Marxism

Periodically I receive letters, one even from a cardinal, inviting me to visit the Third World and see how bad poverty is in the less developed nations. Then, I am assured, I will understand why some American missionaries become involved in Marxist revolutionary movements.

I'm sorry, but I don't accept the validity of the reasoning behind such invitations. Indeed, the invitations demonstrate, it seems to me, the adolescent romanticism that affects many priests and religious from North America who either work in Third World countries or identify such countries from the security of their parishes and schools in America.

To begin with, I have visited many countries in the Third World and am as appalled—indeed, physically overwhelmed—by the poverty as anyone else is, and as profoundly concerned about eliminating that poverty. I do not need my eyes opened to the existence or the horror of contemporary poverty.

(I wonder why so few Third World enthusiasts are concerned about the poverty in the largely unemployed Catholic ghettos of Northern Ireland. I realize the neighborhoods are not quite as bad as Calcutta, but I wonder where the clerical Third World enthusiasts draw the line of their liberation theory so as not to include Belfast.)

There are two problems, however, with the "have your consciousness raised by seeing poverty" argument:

1) To see poverty is not to understand the cause of it. The typical American missionary radical seems to assume that if one visits a Latin American urban slum, one will conclude necessarily and automatically that "the Northern Hemisphere" or "the multinationals" or "the United States" or "the American lifestyle" is the cause of such poverty. They are poor and we are more affluent and therefore we are to blame for their poverty.

In fact, this argument is not self-evidently true at all. Even the Brandt Report—strongly in favor of a transfer of wealth from the Northern Hemisphere to the Southern Hemisphere—does not and cannot, after very careful analysis, accept the explanation that the "North" is responsible for the poverty of the "South." The North, argues the Brandt Report, must do something about the poverty of the South so that the world will not be torn apart, but the North did not cause the South's poverty.

I realize that this response has little effect on missionary radicals. They have surely not read the Brandt Report, probably not even heard of it. One can be horrified by poverty, one can feel responsible to do something about it out of love and/or social justice, but one need not therefore conclude that one has caused it.

2) Nor does it follow, as the missionary radicals seem to take for granted, that the solution to poverty is Marxism. It does not follow for two reasons. First of all, in many Marxist or quasi-Marxist countries, poverty has increased, rather than decreased, after the Communist party has taken over. Mozambique is a good example. Moreover, the food shortages in Poland and the skyrocketing death rate in the Soviet Union ought to be sufficient evidence that Marxism does not cope very well with serious economic problems.

Moreover, there are countries in the world that are anything but Marxist where poverty has either been eliminated or notably diminished. One can mention Ireland and Spain, for example, in the Western world, and Kenya in Africa, and Singapore or Hong Kong and Taiwan in East Asia, and Sri Lanka in South Asia.

The Marxists undoubtedly sound like the most radical of the opponents to poverty, but it does not automatically follow that the most radical solution is the best one. In some circumstances, such may be the case. The implicit argument of the missionary radicals and their supporters that once you've seen poverty you will sympathize with the Marxists simply will not hold water.

I realize that my response is not satisfactory to those who extend me an invitation to come and visit their impoverished communities. It is an argument of logic, of reason, of empirical evidence; none of which, they will argue, will fill the hungry stomach.

Quite possibly not, but then neither will raw, undisciplined emotion or romantic enthusiasm.

Reasons for Not Seeking Revenge

Revenge is never a very good idea—as hard as it is for an Irishman like me to admit that truth. There are excellent reasons for not seeking revenge against Iran for the treatment of the American hostages.

1) Our revenge would not hurt the men and women directly responsible. If there was a way to punish the government leaders—the ayatollah, the prime minister, the "militants" themselves—it might be another matter. They are criminals and should be hauled before an international tribunal. Almost any kind of revenge we try, however, will hurt the innocent along with the guilty,

those who opposed the taking and holding of the hostages as well as those who supported it.

2) Revenge makes us indistinguishable from the Iranians. They took revenge against us for what they imagined to be wrongs. While it is not clear whom they are going to blame for the far worse mess the mullahs are making of the country now that the shah is dead, a revenge response from us lowers their level of morality. They are, in fact, very bad Muslims. That is no reason why we should be very bad Americans.

3) Revenge is a process that never ends, as Palestine and Northern Ireland are ample evidence. It only stops when one side says, "Enough."

Consider the recent shooting of former member of Parliament (the youngest ever) Bernadette Devlin by Protestant extremists. Ms. Devlin is a verbal fire-eater (and a master of the English language as her brilliant autobiography, *The Price of My Soul,* demonstrated) but an apostle of nonviolence. She never harmed anyone herself and never said anything that incited others to do harm. For several years she has been out of Irish and English politics (a loss to both countries) and quietly feeding her husband and raising her three children. Recently she supported the hunger strikers in the British prisons in Ulster.

For that she and her husband were shot at the breakfast table in the presence of their children, though, as she herself observed in her first words on regaining consciousness, they were too tough to kill.

A couple of nights later, self-annointed defenders of Ms. Devlin broke into the home of a Protestant aristocrat and killed the man and his son. Neither victims had anything to do with the Devlin assassination attempt. They were Protestants and aristocrats and that was enough to make them guilty.

Evil? Absurd? Ugly? Criminal? All of those things and more. But that's what revenge leads to.

Now that the hostages are home, we should say "enough" to talk of getting even.

Revenge gives final power to the lowest common denomi-

nator of human nature. It turns control of human affairs to the
killer lying in ambush, the psychopath who delights in killing
the innocent, the torturer who seeks not information but the
pain of others.

In Northern Ireland, revenge has ruled for so long that the
gunmen and the psychopaths have driven out the nonviolent activists like Ms. Devlin and the politicians like Sir Norman
Stronge. Ultimately, British imperialism and colonialism are to
blame. There will be no peace in Ireland until that day when
the English people and the English government finally admit
their guilt—and that day will be long in coming.

Yet revenge against England and against Ulster Protestants
will only delay the day. So too will revenge delay the rebirth of
peace between the people of America and the people of Iran.
Those Americans who are demanding revenge are in their hearts
not very different from the assassins who shot Bernadette Devlin
and killed Sir Norman Stronge.

Sympathizing with Terrorism

Much of the outrage against terrorism is hypocrisy. We are
against terrorists when they are someone else's, but not when
they are our own.

Thus, American left-wing types supported Vietcong terrorism in Vietnam (or at least remained notably silent about it)
and contemporary American right-wing types advocate that the
government contribute to terrorism in Angola and Afghanistan—
against Russians and Cubans, of course. In some fashionable
left-wing circles in the United States and England, PLO terrorism is viewed with mild disapproval at the most, and in the
Third World PLO terrorists are hailed as heroes. American
Catholic radicals support left-wing terrorism in El Salvador
while the Reagan administration currently supports right-wing
terrorism in that battered country. Neither side seems willing to
give the center regime of Colonel Duarte much of a chance. A

fair number of Irish Americans are not affronted by IRA terrorism in Northern Ireland. Israeli Prime Minister Menachem Begin was once a leader in the terrorist group that blew up the King David Hotel in Jerusalem.

I am not saying that all these terrorists are equally bad and I refuse to be sidetracked by casuistic arguments about the relative merits of the various terrorist organizations. Terrorism has become a fact of political life; if we want to eliminate it, we've got to be willing to give up our own terrorists as well as insist that other people give up theirs.

The most simple and fundamental truth about terrorism is that it works—that's why people do it. The IRA invented modern terrorism as a tool in guerrilla warfare during the 1916 uprising. They drove the English out of most of Ireland with their new tactics; in the 1970s their descendants brought down Protestant-dominated regimes in Northern Ireland. Israeli terrorists drove the English out of Palestine. Black terrorists overthrew a white regime in Zimbabwe. Algerian terrorists drove out the French. Turkish terrorists brought down democracy in that beleaguered country. Basque terrorists may yet destroy democracy in Spain. The Tupamaros in Uruguay (enthusiastically endorsed at an international Catholic meeting in 1970) obliterated that country's long tradition of democratic government. The Vietcong drove us out of Vietnam. Greek terrorists forced the English out of Cyprus, only themselves to be shot up by Turkish terrorists. Oh, yes, terrorism works very well indeed. It may be evil, horrifying, terrible and destructive, but it works.

And before Alexander Haig becomes too self-righteous in denouncing international terrorism, he should at least give some explanation of why the United States continues to support the U.N. membership of the Pol Pot regime from Cambodia, a regime that refined terrorism to genocidal proportions.

Professors and intellectuals especially tend to be rather sympathetic to left-wing terrorists and very hostile to right-wing terrorists. The Black Panthers and even the Symbionese Liberation Army, to say nothing of the Weatherpersons, are not without sympathizers in the academic world, and Fidel Castro, who came to power through terrorist tactics, is enthusiastically endorsed by a substantial part of the intelligentsia. Various church organizations cheerfully contribute money to front organizations for African terrorist groups (many of which kill white missionaries), and other church groups, including Catholics, are quite sympathetic to Marxist terrorists in Latin America and even to Puerto Rican terrorists. (Nobody so far as I know has suggested that the church groups might in justice contribute a few dollars to the IRA.)

Indeed, since the death of Gandhi, the only non-terrorist revolutionary movement the world has ignored is Poland. The churches are not contributing to Solidarity and a Polish relief fund. The academic and the liberal left are almost totally silent on the Polish revolution (though *The Nation* recently suggested it was anti-Semitic because of the church's influence—without evidence, of course) and no one is picketing Russian or Polish embassies.

Moral: If you launch a terrorist revolution, there's almost certainly going to be some fashionable group in American society that will support you. If your revolution is nonviolent and would not even consider terrorism as a tactic, then you're on your own.

The Contagious Disease of Terrorism

No useful purpose is served by too closely linking terrorism as a form of political action to the assassination attempts on the pope and the president. The fact that many of the world's political elite enthusiastically approve of terrorism when their side is threatened has created an environment in which the individual crazy can identify his own lunacy with a political cause.

The young Turk who tried to kill the pope is a terrorist in the sense that he was at one time part of a right-wing organization in Turkey. But unlike most of the world's real terrorists, he has no clearly thought-out political ideology. He is not, for example, to be compared with the angry young people of Germany's Baader-Meinhof or the Red Brigades in Italy, which have been spawned in universities and have at least some support from the professoriate in those two countries.

They and their like all over the world have created an environment where the crazies can shoot popes and presidents and thus carve for themselves a place in history. But the two kinds of terrorists are basically different. Aldo Moro was killed by people who, however evil, were basically sane. The pope and the president were shot by madmen with little ideology and no specific goals. The word "terrorist" is predicated on both phenomena only at some risk, obscuring fundamental differences in the problems of dealing with each.

Ideological terrorism (as this column has contended previously) is practiced because it works. Indeed, it is one of the modern world's effective political/military tactics. It has toppled regimes and governments in every continent under heaven. It is the way a small minority can paralyze a society and impose its will on a complacent majority. It may be rigid, doctrinaire, dogmatic and evil, but it is highly effective.

The assassinations that began in Dallas in 1963 are episodes of pointless insanity in which sick people work out their anger on the world and assure themselves permanent fame. Some social scientists think that such random insanity can be compared to an epidemic that spreads around the world, runs its course, then suddenly disappears. The virus was injected into the world by Lee Harvey Oswald and will run an almost inevitable course, perhaps peaking just before its end. Unfortunately, there are no records of similar epidemics in the past because there was never before a world communications system through which the contagion could spread. It may be, however, that the assassination attempts on both the pope and the president within a few short months represent a high point of the epidemic just before it comes to an end.

Such an analysis may explain what happens as madness spreads to madness. Unfortunately, it offers little in the way of suggestion about the antibodies that may resist the contagion. How do you inoculate against an epidemic of assassinations?

One would have been tempted to say that the quick trial and public execution of all such assassins might have cut the epidemic short except that Lee Harvey Oswald was executed very quickly, though without trial. At our present state of understanding how diseased minds affect other diseased minds, the best we can say is that assassins may be discouraged by quick trial and summary execution and that our propensity to provide them with enormous publicity before, during and after their trials aggravates the infection of assassination mania.

Nevertheless, of all the assassins in the last two decades, Lee Harvey Oswald is the only one who is not still alive. The lesson is not lost on the lunatic would-be killers: You can kill or attempt to kill a major public figure and be quite confident that a) you will receive tremendous attention, and b) you will not lose your life.

Under such circumstances, it is small wonder that the mania is contagious: What, if he kills a public figure, does a lunatic have to lose?

Vietnam Vets and
Iranian Hostages

I don't blame the Vietnam vets who are moaning about the nation's manic reaction to the hostage return. I don't think they're guilty of sour grapes at all. The hostages for the most part seemed to have reacted to their captivity with courage and dignity. Yet many soldiers in Vietnam risked their lives every day and did so with courage and patriotism. They are often treated as outcasts; how is it, they may well ask themselves, that the hostages are heroes?

In the objective order there was much greater heroism in Vietnam, yet it is not honored. Indeed, if anything, it is dishonored.

It will not do to say that our presence in Iran was not as immoral as our presence in Vietnam. In both cases the United States was engaged in supporting a weak and incompetent regime which tortured and oppressed many people and which was unpopular to large segments of its population.

Nor will it do to blame the mass media. Even though TV and the press engaged in hostage mania for many weeks, they did so because the hostage story was perceived as one that had captured the spontaneous imagination of the nation. Further, while the reporters and commentators of the national media turned against the Vietnam war early and became, if anything, allies of our enemies, they were able to do so only because the nation was in the process of turning against the war. The poor priest who was a tool of the Iranians is denounced. Jane Fonda, who was a far more willing tool of North Vietnam, wins Academy Awards.

I suspect that history's judgment on both our Iranian and Vietnamese adventures will be remarkably similar. It will not see Vietnam as noble (as Mr. Reagan described it early in the campaign), but neither will it see it as a total evil. In both cases our descendants will say that the United States meant well, that it bungled badly, that it misunderstood the populations with which it was dealing, that it did not know how to be an effective imperial power and that the governments which replaced our clients turned out to be far worse.

Apropos of Vietnam, the judgment will be that the enemy was indeed the enemy but that any strategy that required a half-million American soldiers fighting a land war in Asia was immoral both in its disproportionate use of force and its inevitable failure. On Iran, it will say that we should not have backed a government which was modernizing too rapidly for a devout and archaic people, but that if we were going to back such a government we should not have stopped precisely at the time it most needed our help.

The chaos in Iran proves that the country needs a strong hand. The genocide in Cambodia and against the ethnic Chinese boat people in Vietnam proves that our enemies were every bit as bad as the most militant hawks said they were.

Why, then, incredible enthusiasm for the hostages and indifference if not contempt for the Vietnam vets?

I submit that there are two explanations, neither one of which will bring much consolation to the vets.

National moods change because the nation changes. We are not the same country politically, socially, economically, demographically that we were in 1970. Self-hatred can survive in a nation just so long. Then the country begins to look for symbols that will convert self-hatred back to national pride. The hostages appeared at precisely the right time (though perhaps not from their own personal perspectives) to become symbols for the resurgent national pride and patriotism of which we may arguably have had too much in 1960 and not enough in 1980.

More important was the fact that no one else was being killed in an unpopular cause. Americans turned against the war because of the casualty lists (just as they turned against the Korean war and as they were in the process of turning against World War II when it ended). There were no casualty lists from Iran, save for those who died in the crazy rescue mission (which would have probably killed half the hostages according to the Pentagon computers).

If there had been a massive rescue attempt which led to thousands of deaths and a prolonged war in the mountains of Iran, the hostages would have quickly become very unpopular people.

They were the right people at the right time; the vets were the wrong people at the wrong time. Of course it's not fair, but, as Mr. Cronkite would say, that's the way it was.

A Situation Without Answers

Most Americans understand the situation in Mozambique better than they understand Northern Ireland. Aha, you say, but most Americans know nothing about Mozambique.

Right.

Northern Ireland, your typical American will say, is a place where Protestants and Catholics are fighting one another in a religious war over the reunification of Ireland. Most of the fighting involves extremists on either side and the vast majority of the people on both sides would prefer to have peace.

Virtually every assertion in that paragraph is false. The war in Northern Ireland isn't about religion at all. It's about colonialist oppression. Nor is it about the reunification of Ireland. It is about justice and freedom for the Catholics of the north. Nor is it a conflict involving only extremist minorities, for a very large proportion of both Protestants and Catholics support the extremists. Indeed, a substantial segment of both populations think a continuation of the present conflict is less intolerable than any alternative.

Though many of the ordinary Catholics in Ulster may not be happy with everything the IRA does, the depth of Catholic support for the IRA was revealed in the recent Parliamentary election when a dying hunger striker held without trial in a British prison was elected to the British Parliament in a largely Catholic district.

The dominant political figure of the Protestants, the Reverend Ian Paisley, is very little different from Bobby Sands, the IRA hunger striker. Indeed, in some ways the IRA gunman was more attractive. He was not a pious bigot.

The majority of Catholics are ready to support a Bobby Sands and the majority of Protestants are ready to support an Ian Paisley. The whole situation is one in which there is no political middle, no room for compromise, no possible solution. The IRA will not give up its campaign of violence. The British government will not impose upon the Protestant majority a form of power sharing that would give Ulster some share of justice and freedom in Northern Irish life. Harold Wilson chickened out in 1973 on power sharing, and there is not likely to be another chance in this century.

The characteristic American reaction when faced with a problem is to ask, "Well, what's the answer?"—a question I often hear when I talk about Northern Ireland. The answer is that there is no answer. The conflict between those Northern Irish who call themselves Catholics and those who call themselves Protestants has gone on for a long time and is likely to go on longer.

The only change that would be possible would be a British withdrawal. In such circumstances, the IRA would take over the three Catholic counties and arrange some sort of union with the republic—which would not be at all happy about having to take over those three counties. The Protestant majority in the other three counties would doubtless engage in some medium-scale genocide on the Catholic minority in those counties. Belfast itself, which is part Protestant and part Catholic, would erupt in a violent bloodbath. The army of the republic (the best peace-keeping force in the world, I was told by one of its officers, but not much good at fighting a war) might try to struggle through the Belfast violence to salvage what was left of the Catholics in that city. The best guess is that the army would arrive substantially after the last Catholic had been butchered.

Then there would be peace in Northern Ireland—the peace of the graveyard.

RELIGION

Religion is a given in the human condition. As long as humankind worries about what life means, and as long as most humans have experiences in which life seems to suggest grace or even Grace, there will be religion.

God never died save on divinity school faculties, where he was denied tenure because of an inadequate publication record.

The demoralization of many clergy (of all faiths) who feel that their specific religious role is no longer important and that they must become either bargain-basement therapists or social action activists in order to be relevant is not the result of any development in the world outside of parsonages and rectories. It rather results from reading too many magazines like Commonweal *and* The Christian Century *and too many books by divinity school faculty members.*

There is no such thing as a "modern secular man" who does not need religion.

He too is a product of the Divinity School.

And alas, he was given tenure.

The Great California Monkey Trial

With the usual skill jurists seem to display in such matters, a judge in California has permitted himself to be trapped into hearing a suit that contends that the religious rights of fundamentalist children are being violated by the teaching of evolution in public school classrooms. Unless the thesis of "scientific creationism" is also taught, the plaintiffs charge, there is religious discrimination against fundamentalists.

What about a religion that teaches that the world is flat or that the universe revolves around the earth?

When a presidential candidate, now a president, can remark that he's not altogether sure about evolution, such cases become inevitable. Let's be honest about what they are, however. They are an attempt on the part of religion to dictate scientific findings, an attempt in which the power of the state is invoked to force science to a conclusion it cannot reach on its own.

The Roman church tried that with Galileo and has not recovered yet from its embarrassment.

If a classroom teacher ridicules the faith of those who do not accept the theories of science then he or she is violating the young people's rights to have their religious convictions treated with respect. If he opposes science to the Bible, he is failing in classroom responsibility; the Bible teaches religious truth and science teaches scientific truth and there is no opposition possible because they have different perspectives—as any responsible teacher must know. If a teacher denies the religious truths of the early chapters of the Bible—that God is the lord of creation and that humankind is created in God's image and likeness—then the teacher is using the classroom inappropriately to propound his own religious faith. In each of these cases there is a right to redress either from a school board or—if worse comes to worst—from the courts.

It is the job of science, however, to teach science. Scientific models such as heliocentrism, wave/quantum electromagnetics, molecular biology, DNA genetics and evolution must be taught as the best explanations science has available for the phenomena under its jurisdiction. Those who reject the scientific consensus on these matters for scientific grounds may sometimes be proven right—as Einstein was on Newtonian physics—though only because they come up with a more adequate model as judged by those scientists who are competent to judge.

Those who reject the scientific consensus on religious grounds are surely free to do so, but they have no right to demand that their models be taught as equally valid or equally probable or equally acceptable.

Moreover, by trying to turn the Bible into a book of science, the fundamentalists keep alive the battle between science and religion and discredit all religion. There are only too many secular humanists who are eager to test the Bible against science and find it wanting. In a curious conspiracy both the secularists and the fundamentalists wish to treat Scripture as a book of science, good science according to the latter and bad science according to the former.

The fundamentalists, for all their pride in their biblical fidelity, are guilty of bad Bible knowledge. Indeed, although their natural science is poor, their biblical understanding is even poorer. No responsible or serious biblical scholar today would argue that it was the intent of the author of the first several chapters of Genesis to teach science as we understand the term. He rather pulled together stories and legends that were available to him and that purported to give meaning and purpose to human life (and not a scientific explanation) and then reworked them to teach important religious truths. If asked whether we were descended from prehominids and eventually from some remote common ancestor that we shared with contemporary apes, the Genesis author would doubtless have been horrified and would have been unable to understand the question, much less answer it. If pushed, however, he would have had to reply that he had no idea and that it was not to answer such questions that he wrote his book.

Finally, fundamentalism, in its insistence on the scientific accuracy of a book written before humankind knew what science was, tends to overlook the critical religious truth that creation is good. Since the created world reflects the goodness of God it is sacred and must be reverenced and respected even as God is. The careless and ruthless exploitation of the created world, so typical of the modern age, is far more at odds with the Bible than is even the most radical theory of evolution.

God in the Flicks

God has become a rather important "personality" in American films. Consider: In *All That Jazz*, God was portrayed by Jessica Lange; in *Oh God!* George Burns played the deity; in *Clash of the Titans*, no less a person than Sir Laurence Olivier donned the sacred toga; and more recently, Sir Ralph Richardson was the Supreme Being in *Time Bandits*.

Not bad for God.

Nor were any of the portrayals blasphemous, once you admit that it is not blasphemous for humans to talk of God in any fashion. Surely Sir Ralph as a somewhat hassled but quite "decent" British senior civil servant is no more offensive than the scriptural presentation of God as a desert warrior chieftain.

I personally preferred Ms. Lange; I trust that no one will seriously claim that never before in history has the womanly aspect of God's love been presented in the image of an overwhelmingly attractive girl.

There is one common strain that runs through the four films that is worth considering at Christmas: Each of the "Gods" in the movies is constrained, limited, doing the best he (she) can under very difficult circumstances.

John Denver complains to George Burns about the mess in the world. God replies in a superb theological summary, "I try."

Lord Olivier does his best for the young lovers in *Titans,* but is hemmed in at every turn and only barely manages to triumph over the conspiracies of Olympus.

Ms. Lange hesitates to call Roy Scheider home when she sees the tears of his daughter; yet it is time for him to say his final farewell.

And Sir Ralph, when asked why there is evil, mutters sadly, "Something to do with free will."

God does his/her best, in other words, but the going is often tough and God often has to be content with the limitations and the constraints under which she/he works.

Philosophically, these notions seem quite unacceptable. God is omnipotent, all-powerful; God can do anything he/she wants. There are no limits or constraints on God.

In fact, the revelations of God in the Scriptures seem to suggest rather the opposite. The babe of Bethlehem, the best revelation of God's love we will ever have, certainly experienced limitations and constraints. As Cardinal John Henry Newman said in one of his best Christmas sermons, in Bethlehem we see "the Absolute in swaddling clothes, Omnipotence in bonds."

The "stories of God," in other words, are quite different from the philosophies of God, especially when these philosophies are Greek. The storytellers have no trouble in recording an experience of God in which she/he is perceived as laboring against enormous difficulties in carrying out a plan of love.

In the Scriptures, "omnipotence" has a rather different meaning than it does in philosophy and theology. The word is used nine times in the Book of Revelation, for example, but it does not mean in that book a power which comes from strength or force. Rather, it means a power that comes from persuasiveness. God is able to accomplish his/her plan because of the persuasiveness of her/his love and not because of the capacity to impose on humans whatever he/she wishes.

If you want to preserve Greek philosophy and scholastic theology, you can still do it by asserting that God has chosen to limit himself (and if you are troubled by Greek philosophy and scholastic theology, you will probably resent the "herself") to the constraints imposed by the freedom of natural forces and particularly of human freedom. That's certainly fair enough, though it misses the drama of love we witness every year at this time in Bethlehem.

The flicks, the Scriptures and the Bethlehem scene all tell the same story that our catechisms, our religious education and our sermons often miss: God became "involved," "hooked," infatuated with her/his creation. Much as an author of a novel falls in love with his own creations and then has a terrible time respecting their freedom while he works out his plot, God has fallen for us. His/her omnipotence then becomes an all-powerful persuasive love.

Which is what the crib scene means.

A Religious Classic: All That Jazz

All That Jazz deserved to win the Cannes Film Festival Award. I'd avoided it all winter because a rock musical about death sounded unbearably dreary. The announcement of the award forced me to see it last weekend.

Bob Fosse may not have intended to create a religious classic, but he certainly has done so. His long finale in which death turns into an ecstatic celebration at the end of which the dead man walks down a glowing corridor to meet a gorgeous bride, dressed for her wedding night, is as powerful a commitment to resurrection as I've seen in a long time—even if Fosse doesn't know quite what his symbols mean.

It is also, incidentally, remarkably faithful to the current "death experience" research. Fosse blatantly—but cleverly—footnotes that research, though he is less clear about the biblical origins of his imagery.

Nonetheless, the beautiful bride who plays Death/God is called Angelique—Angel. The notion that death leads to the consummation of a spectacular love affair is throughout the Scriptures, though Christian artists have not quite figured out how to cope with it.

Mystics like John of the Cross and Teresa of Avila have been less reluctant to deal with the eroticism of human/God love than artists and sculptors. Fosse opts for the mystical approach and does the mystics one better by asserting that, for a man, the God who waits at the end of the long tunnel will love like a woman loves.

In fact, the basic plot structure of the film is arranged around what Catholics would call the "particular judgment" of Gideon/Fosse. Angelique/God/Death reviews with him the mistakes, the sins, the failures, the wasted opportunities of his life, chiding him gently but sympathetically and winning from him sorrow for his offenses.

It is almost as though the dialogue is a kind of purgatory the dying man must go through before he is admitted into the bridal chamber.

Many people doubtless thought that *All That Jazz* was tastelessly erotic in its treatment of death and dying. One could debate that point; perhaps some of the scenes were unnecessary. But one has to argue that the Scriptures and the traditions are so filled with erotic imagery to describe the human/God relationship with at worst Fosse went in the right direction but perhaps too far.

I confess that I found his choreographed theology of death and dying as shattering as a retreat. I spent a lot of time the next day praying . . . and not many films have made me do that.

Juxtapose the image of God as Angelique in *All That Jazz* with another God image—Dr. Fischer in Graham Greene's new book, *The Bomb Party.* Greene is an explicitly Christian writer, though one with a permanent dark night of the soul. His God suffers from a broken heart because he is incapable of effectively communicating his love to his wife and daughter. A God whose love is unperceived and unrequited is a legitimate religious vision, too. Fosse and Greene must be seen together and not separately.

But the vision of God as an eager and enticing lover does a lot more for the dreary soul than does the vision of a God as frustrated as the rest of us in his love.

Do I really expect someone as gorgeous and seductive as Angelique to be waiting for me when it comes my turn to walk down that corridor?

If my faith means anything at all, the answer has to be that I expect someone even more spectacularly gorgeous.

Easter Symbols Combine
the Pagan and the Christian

Easter is a pagan feast—in its name and indeed in its symbolism.

In most languages the name of the feast we celebrate this weekend is the same for both its Jewish and Christian versions: Pascha, Pasch, Pasque. In English, however, it still bears the name of the pagan goddess of dawn in Anglo-Saxon mythology, a certain Eostere. This worthy personage was celebrated at the end of the vernal equinox week because in spring dawn came earlier every morning and the days were longer than the nights.

There were some special symbols associated with the goddess Eostere—rabbits, eggs and lilies.

Fifteen hundred years after the Angles and the Saxons came into the Christian fold, we still have the name of their equinox festival and we still have bunnies, eggs and lilies. The Anglo-Saxon spring symbols celebrated the rebirth of life in springtime. They still do, though now in a thoroughly Christian context. So too dawn is honored, the dawn of a new day of freedom and hope.

The pagan layers that have been absorbed into a Christian and Jewish context go back long before the Angles and the Saxons and the Jutes, however. The three main images of the Passover—unleavened bread, paschal lamb and fire and water—are all pagan symbols. The first two were pre-Sinai Semitic spring festival themes—the paschal lamb coming from a grazing culture and the unleavened bread from a farming culture. The fire and the water, more vividly present in the Christian Passover than in the Jewish one, are part of a Roman spring ceremony added to the Christian liturgy in the fourth century.

All represent fertility; that is to say, they all represent life and the triumph of spring life over the death of winter. The fertility there of the candle and the water is particularly obvious since in virtually all pagan religions a lighted candle represents maleness and water femaleness. The plunging of the candle into the water represents the marriage union from which new life comes. One of the formulae the priest may use at this time leaves no doubt about the meaning: "May this candle fructify these waters."

The pagan symbols have been reinterpreted, of course: The union of the candle and water now is said to represent the love of God for his people. But note that just as in the reinterpretation of eggs and lilies, the basic meaning of the symbol, its fundamental structure, is not altered. It is, rather, placed in a new context and seen to mean not less than it once did, but more.

There are a number of conclusions that might be drawn from the remarkable durability of pagan symbols within a Christian (or Jewish) context. First of all, we moderns ought to have a lot more humility than we do on the subject of our pagan ancestors. They were not religious barbarians. We are their descendants culturally and religiously, as well as biologically. We ought to be much more conscious than we are of our debt to them. If it wasn't for the Angles and the Saxons, we would have neither the Easter Bunny nor the Easter lily.

Second, the problem of adapting native cultural practices that is troubling the Roman Curia in Africa is essentially a false problem. During Holy Week the churches celebrate Christian feasts filled with pagan symbols. There was a time when the church was not afraid of absorbing pagan customs. A mistaken notion that Christianity requires European forms and behavior is a nontraditional violation of the basic insight that Christianity is strong enough to absorb anything. However, if Christianity is not weak and does not need to be protected at all times from the threat of pagan contamination (a possibility that would have amused those who put the sexual ritual of fire and water into the Easter service), then you don't need a Roman Curia snooping around to control and protect Christianity.

Finally, while not all religions are the same, there are strong continuities in human religious experiences. Doctrines are different, and that is important; but pictures and images and stories are similar and that is more important.

Is God Permissive?

There is a dramatic change in religious sensibility going on among young Americans. It is accompanied by an equally dramatic change in their life values and expectations. But the two changes seem to be contradictory.

Teenage Americans, according to the best survey data currently available, are much less permissive in their sexual attitudes than young people just a few years older—and less permissive than many of their parents. However, their imagery of God is much more affectionate, tolerant and permissive than that of older generations, even the older generation just ahead of them.

Teens are much more likely than older people to picture God as tolerant, tender, gentle and loving. They are also more likely to think of God as a mother and a lover. Moreover, this change of religious sensibility—which, if it is permanent, will transform religion in decades to come—does not appear to be a life-cycle phenomenon that will diminish as they grow older. Rather, it seems like an authentic generational effect, attributable to experiences (particularly in their relationships with their mothers) that are likely to have a powerful long-run impact on their religious and personal lives—an effect which seems to be totally benign.

I realize that it is unfashionable to say anything nice about teenagers or their mothers these days. One is supposed to think that everything is going wrong in the American family. Nonetheless, as far as religious sensibility is concerned some things are going right—unless you happen to be a Catholic bishop or a Moral Majority TV preacher and reject the image of a tender compassionate God.

On the other hand, in seeming contradiction, teens are more likely than their immediate predecessors to value highly virginity and chastity and to be opposed to premarital sex—a kind of sexual revolution in reverse. How can you have more permissive images of God and less permissive sexual attitudes?

When I lecture on the new religious sensibility, there is always some right-wing Catholic nut in the audience who demands to know whether the new religious sensibility is not responsible for "all the immorality" among the young. Isn't there, the righteous nut asks eagerly, a correlation between a permissive God and sexual promiscuity?

It's one of those situations you dream about. I say yes there is and the flake's eyes light up. I add it is a negative correlation—the stronger your image of a tender and affectionate God, God as mother and lover, the less likely you are to approve of permissiveness.

The expression on the fanatic's face indicates that he/she is going to write a letter to Rome about me. Another letter, that is.

I suppose the reason for the negative correlation is that if you are aware in your imagination that you are caught up in a love affair with God you are a little more careful about your human love affairs. Or maybe you value yourself more highly and are less likely to turn yourself into a thing.

There is little consolation for the pope and his docile bishops in these findings: Even those young Catholics with the strongest images of a God of love reject the church's teachings on birth control and divorce. Nevertheless, if the pope wishes to win young Catholics away from premarital sex, the best thing he can do is to insist strongly on the image of a tender, affectionate and loving God. Warnings or denunciations won't do it. A God who is a passionate lover will.

Just now there is little sign of such a God in the harsh, unforgiving, repressive Catholic Church.

The correlation between an image of a loving God and a

return to sexual values is also a judgment on those religious "liberals" who thought that in the name of love you had to throw out all traditional values. They made the same mistake that the pope and the bishops make. It is a very old mistake.

Despite the "liberals" and the Neanderthals, however, love and promiscuity are not the same thing.

Are Biblical Stories About God?

If an anthropologist from outer space should arrive on the planet Earth to do field work on earthly religions, I'm sure he would say that one of the most striking aspects of the Jewish and Christian Scriptures is that they are filled with stories that don't really seem to be very religious at all. What kind of religion is it, the three-eyed, green-bodied Martian anthropologist would demand, that is preoccupied with secular stories?

For example, he would say, I am fully prepared to admit that the stories of David and Joseph in the Jewish Scriptures are brilliantly written artistic creations, marvelously ingenious stories of human love and human hatred, filled with profound characterizations and poignant conflict. But, after all, they don't really say much about God, do they?

And, he might go on, Jesus was truly a storyteller of incomparable color. His parables are masterpieces, brilliant little gems to unnerve, disconcert, challenge and open up new possibilities. But they're not very religious, are they? They seem to be about kings going on journeys and merchants poking around bazaars and rich men having wedding parties and young ne'er-do-wells coming back to calm their fathers and spendthrift farmers who pay full day's wages to those who only work for an hour or two. Entertaining anecdotes, devastating challenges, but where is God in all of these stories? Are not the parables of Jesus marvelous miniature accounts of the ambiguities and the dilemmas, the hopes and the fears of everyday life?

This "otherworldly" perspective helps us to face candidly

something that most of us barely seem to notice: The Scriptures, both Jewish and Christian, are very secular books. They are stories which are as secular and often as shocking as those which one can find on the bestseller lists.

Professor Robert Alter, in his new book, *The Art of Biblical Narrative,* has dramatically demonstrated that the stories in the Jewish Scriptures are told with masterful literary skill by authors who had to have been accomplished practitioners of the narrative arts. They are for the most part, however, not stories directly or explicitly about God. Similarly, the parables of Jesus do not deal directly with God either, but with the conflicts of human life.

In both cases, of course, the storytellers intend to open up to those who read or listen or hear the story the possibility of a different kind of life that results from a highly specific notion of God and God's love. The stories in the Scriptures are thoughts with religious and ethical challenges, but both the challenge and the God who presents the challenge are not "morals" added on to the story; they are possibilities structured into the very nature of the story. You don't have to explain the parable. You don't have to explain the story of Joseph. Rather, you tell the story and the ones who hear it intuitively and instinctively know what kind of God is lurking behind the story.

Alter contends that modern fiction is rooted in the storytelling of the Scriptures. The artful tales of the Jewish and Christian Scriptures prepared the Western culture for prose fiction. And the best writers even today do write with powerful moral vision, but visions that are structured into the stories and not tacked on at the end.

Those who object to us storytellers when we deal with the human condition as it is, instead of describing an edifying and pious human condition as it ought to be, should go back and look at the stories in the Scriptures. Challenging, disconcerting, upsetting tales they may be, but neither the parables of Jesus nor the tales of David and Joseph in the Old Testament are pious or edifying.

A Conversation with
St. John the Divine

In the caves of Dalkey, in South County Dublin, as the Irish
writer Flan O'Brien has told us, one can on certain days talk to
famous men out of the past. O'Brien himself had a long talk in
one of the caves with Saint Augustine.

More recently, I encountered Saint John the Divine in the
same cave. He was a young fellow with long blond hair and arms
like telephone poles, a pro lineman, a sort of younger Merlin
Olsen.

"You are in great trouble, you are, Saint John the Divine,"
said I, "and you are an evangelist."

"You mean with that fella Ray Brown? Well, let me tell you
a thing or two about how that book was really . . ."

"I don't mean that at all, at all. I'm referring to the terrible
things you said about the magisterium in your book. Do you
realize how much comfort you give to the enemies of the church
and how many young people will leave the church because of
your portrait of the hierarchy?"

"I take your point," said he. "You're using against me the
same argument that my colleague, the bishop of Disney World,
is using against you: It will hurt the faith to describe bishops as
men with human weaknesses and failings."

"Indeed yes," said I. "It shocks the laity and drives those
on the margins out of the church."

"Well, the problem with you is that you don't understand
the way things change. You see, in our day, the hierarchy was a
pretty scruffy lot. Peter, poor old man, was a loudmouth brag-
gart. And Thomas shot his mouth off a lot, too. Me and my
brother, God forgive us for it, were hot-tempered and ambitious.
Simon the Zealot was a zealot, and no good ever came from that.
And Judas was no good at all, at all.

"But since then, there has been a considerable upgrading of the quality of the leadership, if you follow me; with bishops like the three G-men, you have a different situation altogether."

"G-men?"

"Sure," said Saint John the Divine, "Gerety, Grady and Gelineau. With men of such integrity, wisdom and virtue, there's every reason in the world to have the faithful depend on a bishop's personal goodness and intelligence for their faith. The trouble with you is that you haven't kept up with the changing times."

"Are you trying to tell me that the apostolic delegate is better at picking bishops than Himself was?" I demanded.

"That's exactly what I'm saying," insisted Saint John the Divine. "Himself was kind of careless about those things. He sure picked a crowd of us who weren't safe at all, at all. Seemed to think that his father's love made up for our weaknesses. Now, I ask you, is that any way to run a church?"

"I can't believe you mean these things," I said sadly.

"I didn't say I meant them." He favored me with a wink. "I'm saying them for the record; I wouldn't want anyone writing a letter about me to Rome. Something like that gets in your file and you don't have much chance of making cardinal."

"Was Peter married?" I asked, changing the subject.

"I won't comment on that at all," he said sharply. "The fella that scribbled down those lines about Peter's mother-in-law was a Communist plotter. Remember what your man in Philadelphia —your Philadelphia, not the one I wrote the Book of Revelation for—said when it was reported that this Polish fella had been married? Well, if I said anything about Ms. Peter, he'd be calling me a Communist agent, too. I'll tell you one thing, though: The poor woman had to be a saint to put up with a husband like Peter, and himself a pope, too."

"This conversation has not gone the way I thought it would," I said sadly.

"Well, then, let me ask a question. Your man in Florida who took out after you, sure I can understand that. What if the apostolic delegate found out that he was the one who set you to writing in the first place? But he did say that he thought your portrait of 'warm sexuality' would lead young people to commit sin . . ."

"He said that indeed."

"I've been around for a long time," said Saint John the Divine, "and to tell you the truth, I've never heard of cold sexuality. Tell me, do they have that variety in the great state of Florida?"

"In Disney World they do."

The Failure of Sin, Morality, Religion

What would be the increase in the fornication rate, I asked a priest with vast pastoral experience, if the church should announce tomorrow that fornication was only a venial sin?

It wouldn't change at all, replied my colleague.

The conversation was based on a remark in an article on the Borgias (in response to a BBC series on those colorful representatives of the magisterium of the past) in the London *Tablet*. Historian E. E. Y. Hales noted, in passing, that when Alexander was pope and Cesare was a cardinal and an archbishop, sins of the flesh were considered to be only venial.

Now, let me quickly note that I am not saying that fornication is only a venial sin, though I think there was a time in the past when a lot of laity and some clergy in many parts of the Catholic world did not consider it as serious as we do today.

My point is that even on its own terms, the sin-morality approach to religion is not effective today and probably never has been. You can tell people that certain forms of behavior are mortally sinful, but that does not mean they won't engage in such behavior. The birth control pill may have changed many "incomplete" sins of fornication (read "necking and petting") to "complete" sins, but it is to be doubted that the fear of mortal sin and of hellfire has kept many young people (and older people too) in line when the hormones were operating.

In actual practice, Catholicism has become for most of its members in this country and many of its teachers and leaders a mixture of papal power and sexual morality. Indeed, in the questionnaire sent out about men who are being considered for the hierarchy, three "doctrinal" questions are asked—birth control, celibacy and the ordination of women.

It would be interesting historically to determine how this reduction of Catholicism to sex and power—and more recently a bizarre equation of sexual morality with papal power—has occurred. Surely those are not the principal concerns of the New Testament or the fathers of the church. And surely there is much more to Catholicism.

Whatever the origins of this curious narrowing of Catholicism to a couple of issues that in the past would have been considered peripheral (and the angry letters I will receive from conservatives in response to this statement will only prove my point), the fact remains that even in terms of its own goal of preventing people from committing "sins of the flesh," mortal-sin Catholicism does not work.

Moreover, the evidence is that, among American Catholics, acceptance of both the sexual ethic and papal authority is at an all-time low.

Jesus tried to motivate those who came to hear him, not by talking of mortal sin, but by revealing God's love and insisting on the urgency of responding to God's love. In the Book of Revelation, the word "omnipotence" is used nine times, each time to refer not to force or authority, but to the persuasiveness of love.

Recent research on young adults demonstrates that young people avoid sexual sin, not because it is sin but because they have strong religious images of a tender and loving God and great respect for one another. They are, in other words, motivated precisely by the appeals that Jesus used and not by the appeals that many church leaders and teachers substitute for the motivations of the Scriptures.

I am not suggesting that we "change" our teaching about

the sinfulness of certain actions. What I am suggesting is that if we want Catholics to avoid sins of the flesh, the principal motivation to offer them is the same one Jesus offered: Love. One searches in vain in the ordinary teaching of the official church in these areas for any realization that, while the fear of the Lord is the beginning of wisdom, it is only the beginning.

Jesus' Divinity Needs to Keep Its Perspective

Is the greater danger that Christians will deny the humanity of Jesus or the divinity of Jesus? If one pays any attention to the witch-hunts currently being conducted by the Vatican, then the humanity of Jesus is not in jeopardy. The real danger is from modern "existential" theologians who want to deny the divinity of Jesus.

Historically, just the opposite has been the case. The principal concern of the church through the centuries has been to protect the humanity of Jesus from those who would have turned him into the *theos aner* of Greek mythology. Indeed, at most times in the long Christological conflicts, the preservation of the humanity of Jesus turned out to be a very near thing indeed.

The Congregation for the Defense of the Faith would persuade us that in the last century, rationalism, materialism, secularism, etc., have reversed with the tide and that the faith must be defended against attempts of secular humanists and the historical critical methods to turn Jesus into someone "purely human."

There is something to be said for this position. *Godspell* and *Jesus Christ, Superstar* are clearly and obviously attempts to reduce Jesus to a "purely human" level. They fail as artistic works, incidentally, precisely for this reason.

However, one could also make the opposite case. If secu-

lar culture does indeed reduce Jesus to the merely human, it
has always done so ever since the days of the Roman Empire.
May not the real danger to Christology still be what it has always
been: The tenacious insistence of some theologians, religious
teachers and purveyors of popular piety to diminish substantially, if not utterly obviate, the humanity of Jesus?

This thought occurred to me again as I was reading the
Reverend Michael Cook's excellent book, *The Jesus of Faith*.
Cook quite correctly argues that Jesus is God's word—the full-
est revelation of what humanity is which will ever be made and
which indeed can ever be made. It is precisely, according to
Cook, in the full humanity of Jesus that God's word can be
spoken. Deprive Jesus of his humanity and you deprive God's
word of its impact. Diminish the humanity of Jesus and you
diminish the impact of the Word. To rephrase the same perspective in the words of the Council of Chalcedon, if you diminish the humanity of Jesus, you diminish the divinity too. It is
only by fully asserting the humanity that you are able to fully
reveal the divinity.

The fathers of the Council of Chalcedon caught this
paradox. It has to be said, however, that many of those who
have interpreted the council—including some of Father Schillebeeckx's judges—have not comprehended it at all. To put the
matter a little differently, the contest between the humanity
and the divinity that both the hyper-orthodox and the hyper-
rationalists would impose upon it obscures completely the
paradox of the Incarnation, a paradox which must absolutely be
preserved if one wishes to comprehend Jesus. The more fully
human we see Jesus, the more adequately divine he becomes
for us.

One of the incredibly charming aspects of the character of
Jesus is his courtesy, fairness, respect and friendship for women.
Jesus' attitude toward women was utterly and completely un-
characteristic of his age. Jesus liked women, he respected them,
he treated them as equals—traits which now, as then, were
admirably and delightfully human, but which also revealed
spectacularly God's word on the subject of sexual equality and
God's equal love for both men and women. No "mere" man of
his age could possibly have related to women the way Jesus did.

It is then precisely in the humanity of his attitude toward women that we discover also the hint of the divinity, the hint of God's word.

I am not sure how successful all the new Christological attempts are, not because I think that men like Schillebeeckx or Cook are weakening the faith, but because I believe that their necessarily philosophical approach is not comprehensible to most laity or clergy. The work that such theologians are doing is necessary, but I'm afraid not sufficient.

I would like to suggest that along with the theological study of Christology there also ought to be a sociological Christology. It seems to me that the Christian faithful have been remarkably successful through the centuries in tenaciously holding to the paradox of Jesus, despite assaults from both the right and the left. If the "sense of the faithful" is a legitimate theological "locus"—and despite recent attempts of Roman theologians to minimize it, nobody has denied that it is—and if one is seriously engaged in a "Christology from below," then ought not one to try to determine how the "faithful" and those in the "below" think of, picture and imagine Jesus?

The research my colleagues and I have done on the religious imagination of the young Catholic adult (published by William H. Sadlier) might represent a youthful beginning. Surely there can be no doubt after reading our data that for Catholics under fifty, Jesus is truly what Father Cook says he is: The sacrament of God's love among us.

Whatever Happened to Pilgrimages?

Since the reforms of the Second Vatican Council, Roman Catholics have pretty much abandoned their practice of marching around the countryside to shrines, right?

And Protestants, never given to the popish practice of pilgrimages, have heaved a sigh of relief, right?

Wrong on both counts.

The various Roman Catholic shrines around the world, especially those in honor of Mary, the mother of Jesus—Knock, Lourdes, Fatima, even the monstrosity on the Catholic University campus in Washington—report record crowds each year. The Polish shrine of Jasna Gora (Glowing Mountain), where the Black Madonna is honored, may be the most important symbolic resource supporting the Polish Revolution.

And in France, Protestants pilgrimage to the monastery at Taize, staffed, interestingly enough, by Protestant monks.

Perhaps the most astonishing of all the shrines is Walsingham, in England, where the mother of Jesus was honored for almost a thousand years. Then the shrine was leveled during the Reformation and, as Hilaire Belloc lamented in an eloquent poem, no longer did pilgrims' feet walk the road to Walsingham.

Belloc was wrong, however. Even as he wrote, the Anglican vicar at Walsingham was quietly opening a new shrine. Later, a Roman Catholic shrine would be added, first in competition and now in ecumenical cooperation. On the fiftieth anniversary of the new Walsingham, the archbishops of Canterbury and Westminster and leaders of many of the Free Churches led an ecumenical pilgrimage across the flat Norfolk countryside to honor Our Lady of Walsingham, who survived the Reformation after all and now presides over the ecumenical age.

So what's with pilgrimages?

Professor Christian Zacher, in a book called *Curiosity and Pilgrimage*, shows that in the Middle Ages one went on pilgrimage (as did Chaucer's pilgrims) in part because it was an exciting adventure. So too today we go to Rome or Lourdes or Knock because they're something to talk about when we go home.

Yet no one goes to Walsingham or Catholic U or Jasna Gora out of curiosity. And if you're Irish, you don't go to Knock just to say you've been there. Nor if you're Mexican do you visit Guadalupe (which celebrated its four-hundred-fiftieth anniversary some time ago, by the way), so you can come home and talk about it.

Curiosity, adventure, excitement, the prospect of fascinating memories—all are part of the pilgrimage syndrome, but there's more that has to be said.

Mecca, Lourdes, Guadalupe, Jasna Gora, even Knock are sacred places, so designated by popular acclaim, no matter what scholars may think of the events that are alleged to have occurred in these holy locations. People visit them because there is a powerful need in the human personality to set aside some places as "special," as linked to the ultimate purposes, as both "fascinating and terrifying" (in the words of the German sociologist Rudolph Otto).

A lot of progressive theologians and religious thinkers wrote this propensity off in the last couple of decades. We had become "secularized"; sacred time and sacred place were no longer needed. They were relics of the "mythological" past.

Such "experts" were not very perceptive. Even that most secularist of states, the Soviet Union, had to turn Lenin's tomb into a shrine.

If there is purpose in human life—and most people persist in believing that there is, regardless of what philosophers and professors try to tell them—then it is not at all unreasonable to suppose that there are certain places in the world where one can come in special contact with such purpose, or, if one wishes, Purpose.

Moreover, if enough of us believe that and go to such places, it will turn out that we come back with our sense of purpose and faith renewed. Our conviction that a place is fascinating and terrifying in fact makes it so—even 350 years after it has been destroyed (as was Walsingham) by those who thought they were eliminating forever such foolish superstition.

This week, around the world, millions of people will march to Guadalupe, Knock, Jasna Gora, Lourdes and even Walsingham to honor a young Jewish woman who bore a manchild. Not all of them will be Roman Catholics by any means.

You may be affronted by such behavior. That is your right.

But don't think that is ever likely to stop.

Being Religious Means More Than Going to Church

"It's as difficult to stop being Catholic as it is to stop being black," said novelist John R. Powers on a recent TV program, "and that has nothing to do with the church."

The gifted young author of *The Last Catholic in America* and *Do Black Patent Leather Shoes Really Reflect Up?* was stating in concrete terms an important distinction that applies not only to Catholicism but to most other religious traditions: A religion is both a heritage and an institution. Of the two, heritage is the more pervasive in its influence and more durable.

You may be able to break away from the institution and even join another one. The heritage, however, is likely to maintain its influence on you even though you think you've broken free of it. It doesn't matter whether you are a Catholic or a Jew or a Lutheran or a Southern Baptist or a Mormon or a Greek Orthodox. You may well have disaffiliated yourself from the institution and you may well have repudiated many of its formal doctrines, but the pictures and the images and the stories (and maybe even the relationships) that constitute religious heritage hang on and persist in your imagination no matter how hard you try to get rid of them. The wise person does not so much escape from his/her heritage as make peace with it.

Much of the thinking and talking about religion that goes on, especially among well-educated people, assumes that religion is the doctrines that you believe in and the church with which you are affiliated. But the serious research that has been done on religion by sociologists, theologians, psychologists and historians in recent years suggests that the raw power of religion, its attractiveness, its influence, its pervasiveness, has little to do with creedal propositions and institutional affiliations, and much to do with songs and stories and pictures and ceremonies which are powerfully imprinted on one's imagination very early in life, especially in the family environment. It is not religious doctrine and not even the institutional church, for example, that provides the Catholic power which supports the Solidarity trade movement in Poland. It is hymns and prayers and images of the Madonna and a thousand years of Polish Catholic tradition.

Among young American Catholics, attitudes toward sexual morality are not so much affected by what they believe about the bishops or about the pope, but by their pictures of Jesus, Mary and God. Young people who think of God as passionately loving are much less likely to approve of sexual promiscuity. Whether they think the pope is infallible is irrelevant; whether they picture God as a mother or a lover is very important indeed.

Most religious leaders are willing to concede some importance to the imaginative end of religion, though perhaps not very much. For them what counts is that you profess affiliation to the institution and that you accept all its teachings and rules. The pictures, images and stories are a kind of holdover from the pre-rational past, to be tolerated, perhaps, but not taken seriously.

In fact, the opposite seems to be the case. Religion has survived a long time without too much in the way of either formal doctrines or formal institutions, and it seems to survive very well today quite independent of both of them. I do not want to suggest that doctrines or institutions are unimportant, but rather that it would appear they are much less important than such things as the Passover service, a Lutheran hymn, a Catholic Midnight Mass or First Communion or May Crowning.

A Time to Keep on Hoping

This is the time of Spring Festival or Easter, the Passover, May Day, and—if there are any Druids still around—Beltaine. Each of the festivals in their own way celebrates the unquenchable hopefulness of human nature.

The key religious question is not whether we hope or even whether we celebrate hope. The answers to those questions are obvious. Rather, the question is whether we can trust our propensity to hope. Is it a revelation or a deception?

The themes of the various spring festivals are similar. Indeed—as I wrote in another piece—in most languages the Jewish feast of Passover and the Christian feast of Easter have the same name.

The feasts all assert one way or another the primacy of life over death, of freedom over slavery, of rebirth over despair. Beltaine, May Day, Easter, all celebrate sacred trees that united earth and heaven and around which we dance in festive celebration. Easter and Passover have sacred banquets that represent our unity with each other and with the Source of our Hope. Both Jewish and Christian celebrations also speak of fire and water as the origins of life.

It was the passage through the waters of the Red Sea, led by the pillar of fire, that freed the Hebrews and made them a people. Similarly, in the Easter Vigil service of Catholic Christianity the fire representing the love of God revealed in Jesus and the waters representing humankind are dramatically combined to produce the new life which is God's people.

Most of these rites in their origins had a strong fertility implication. Spring is the time when the fruits of the fields and the fruits of the flocks are produced by the lifegiving energies of fertility. Humankind has always believed that fertility and sexuality are a defiance of the powers of death. In old Irish times, couples would have sexual intercourse in the fields outside of a house in which a wake was being held. In the very modern and up-to-date television series *United States,* the couple, having explained death to their children and then wrestled with it themselves, make love before they enter the funeral limousine to go to the burial of a dead relative.

The spring festivals, then, are a time when life is reborn, when hope is renewed and when love can be revitalized precisely because there is life and hope. I am not suggesting that all the festivals have the same substantive content, though Easter and Passover reveal the same loving and liberating and implacably faithful deity.

Rather, I am suggesting, purely from the social science viewpoint, that the imaginative structures of our spring festivals are remarkably similar. They all shout at death with Saint Paul: "O Death, where is thy sting? O Grave, where is thy victory?"

Most scholars who have studied the matter think that hope is innate in our personality, perhaps genetically programmed. Spring festivals are a challenge to us whether we are willing to keep on hoping, no matter how much seems to be wrong.

MARRIAGE, FAMILY & SEX

"At our age," a gorgeous Irish redhead in her early forties said to me the other day, "most of us know that sex is crucial in keeping the glow in marriage. And we even have a pretty good idea what that means in terms of technique. If we don't, we can find the books which will tell us. The real problem is motivation. We're not sure it's worth the effort, the risk, the work, the possible humiliation. Why doesn't the church provide us with motivation? Isn't that what religion is for?"

Indeed yes. But the church is more interested in warning, wringing its hands, and exhorting the laity to avoid unbridled passion.

When everyone one knows (who doesn't live in the Vatican or in the Vatican enclaves called chancery offices) says that the problem in human love is bridled passion.

The great failure of the church is not the insensitivity of the birth control encyclical. The great failure is the nonrecognition of the spiritual and ascetic dimensions of married sex.

And I don't mean the spirituality of not having sex or not enjoying it much when you do have it. After a while, that takes no spiritual motivation at all. I mean the spirituality of celebrating sex and keeping love alive with it.

That failure, in centuries to come, will rank with the Galileo caper.

Kramer vs. Kramer
Touches Real-life Marriages

One hears that there is going to be a sequel to *Kramer vs. Kramer* in which a reconciliation, vaguely hinted at the end of the film, actually occurs. It would be the final cliché in a cliché-ridden drama (though one which is still several cuts above the typical shopping-mall entertainment these days).

It would also complete the remarkable paradigm for the first decade of American marriage which the film portrays. When clichés turn into paradigms we face puzzle, bafflement and mystery.

The divorce of the Kramers took place in the eighth year of the marriage. The wife says on the witness stand that it was a happy marriage for two years (though can one imagine any youthful American professional man in this day and age refusing to let his wife work after marriage—or a professional woman accepting such a refusal?). The glimmers of reconciliation are to be seen in the ninth year. If it works, the tenth year will be moderately happy, perhaps even better than the first two.

I watched the film in stunned amazement because a group of colleagues and I have just finished documenting the same cycle in the marriages of American young people (Catholics in this case, but they probably are no different in this respect from other Americans). Like most other researchers we noted in our sample the decline of marital satisfactions after the second year together—in everything from finances to sex. We also discovered that a very large number of marriages (between one third and one half, depending on which indicator you watch) hit rock bottom during the seventh and eighth year—just as did the union of Mr. and Ms. Kramer.

Then, however, in the ninth and tenth year there is a remarkable rebound, so that a higher proportion of young couples are happier in their relationship at the end of the decade than at the beginning.

The amazing phenomenon is not the decline in marital satisfaction—there are plenty of reasons to explain that. The astonishing fact is the rebound—for which there are no explanations that I have heard. Indeed, I cannot find in the marriage literature any discussion or even awareness of the rebound—though after we did our analysis I learned from many married friends that they had experienced just such a cycle in their marriages.

We do know that during the last two years of the first decade of a Catholic marriage there is a remarkable improvement in the quality of the religious imagery of both the husband and wife. God, Jesus, Mary—are all imagined as much warmer, more gentle and more patient. Whether that change is a cause or an effect is impossible to say. Since we were unprepared to find the marriage cycle, we had no questions in the study which would enable us to test an explanation.

At the risk of sounding corny, I would speculate that the reason might be the enormous residual power of love—an explanation which seems to have occurred to the makers of *Kramer vs. Kramer*, too.

I draw two conclusions, one for marriage education and one for research.

Young people are told before marriage that they will have to deal with a period of "adjustment." My impression is that they are led to think that this will take a few months or a year at the most. We ought to tell them that it will take more like eight years, that a few of those years can be very rough and that there will be powerful resources in their relationship which can see them through the difficult times.

My research conclusion is that a lot more money and energy should be expended on studying the development of marital intimacy than is presently being spent. What, for example, is one to make of the parallel and related cycles of religious imagery?

Such research will not be funded either by the federal government or the major private foundations, since the anti-family veto groups have been able to kill all such projects. By definition, for these folks, marriage and family can't work. Thus it would seem that church groups (like the Knights of Columbus, who funded our project) will have to fill the vacuum. Given the possibilities implicit in *Kramer vs. Kramer* becoming paradigmatic, I should think they would be willing and eager.

Rediscovering the Role of Marriage

Life with commitments looks hard until one considers the alternatives.

I heard a story the other day about a woman in her thirties who had drifted from love affair to love affair since college graduation, steadfastly refusing to make any long-term commitments to anyone. Then she encountered a man whom she found more attractive than any of the others, but who somehow did not seem ready to respond to her hint that it would be acceptable for him to move in.

Finally, almost in desperation, she suggested explicitly that he share her apartment. The man responded: "No, I won't live with you. I swore after my last experience of five years in such a relationship that I'd never do it again. I'll marry you, though, if you want. I'd like that very much."

Much to her surprise, the woman discovered that she would like it very much, too.

The generation that thought it discovered out-of-wedlock relationships is now in the process of discovering marriage. The generation that said that long-term commitments aren't necessary is discovering that long-term commitments may be a very good idea. The generation that wrote off ceremonies of public commitment as meaningless rituals has discovered that when difficulties and tensions arise in intimate relationships, a memory of public commitment provides the resources and the motivations that are necessary to overcome the problems and avoid the pain of shattered intimacies.

So it turns out that shattered intimacies do hurt terribly and that publicly and ritually celebrated commitments help preserve intimacy precisely at those times when it comes dangerously close to being shattered.

One rejoices that the importance of commitment has been rediscovered, but one laments the enormous cost in suffering and heartache that has been required for the rediscovery. Why was it necessary to write off all the accumulated wisdom of the past? Why was it necessary to discover, completely alone, that commitments make life easier, not harder, as though no one who has ever lived before us was ever aware of such wisdom?

Let me suggest that, in addition to the narcissism of those who grew up between 1965 and 1975, two explanations for this phenomenon have to do with the abject failure of the churches.

First of all, much of organized religion has been so legalistic in its approach to sex and marriage that ordinary people think that the traditions are purely arbitrary and have no basis in human wisdom or experience. You shouldn't live together without the benefit of marriage because that's what the laws say, that's what the rules demand, and not because the accumulated wisdom of human experience shows that long-term commitments make powerful reinforcements of human love.

Natural law, in the Catholic tradition, is a law because it is natural and does not become natural because it is the law. The nature of human nature and the wisdom of human experience shape the law, but many of us who were raised in the church of the thirties and forties and fifties were taught just the opposite: The law shapes human nature. Human nature exists to serve the law, instead of being served by it.

Moreover, most religions have never tried seriously to distinguish between the transmission of property and legal contracts aspects of traditional marriage and the interpersonal wisdom in that institution. At one time, marriage was not merely the union between two people, but an arrangement for the transmission of property between two families. It is necessary to sort out the interpersonal wisdom from the property transmission custom of traditional marriage.

This will be a very difficult task, since for most of history the two have been inextricably linked. Those churches that have insisted on the importance of marriage and family have refused to do what is necessary to underscore the traditional wisdom. They, rather, have been content to lay down the law in all its old, rigid, legalistic and unnuanced terminology. A couple of generations of young people heard the law and missed the wisdom.

Now they are discovering on their own, the hard way, the wisdom that was obscured by the law. Let us be candid about it: The churches failed and the churches will continue to fail young people if they continue, like the liberal church, to throw out the baby of wisdom with the bathwater of law, or, like the conservative church, to be so concerned about legalistic bathwater as to be hardly aware that the baby exists.

What Parents Are Missing

The other day I bumped into a former colleague who, looking pretty much like a teenager herself, has suddenly discovered that she has a teenager in her family. She reported that she found it an enormously enjoyable experience.

"Of course," she added, "it isn't easy. It takes a tremendous amount of work. You have to put in almost as much effort with a teenager as you do with a husband. The parent-teenager thing is pretty near as hard as the husband-wife thing."

The wisdom of that observation jolted me. When we are young most of us are victims of the easy romanticism which says that once you've fallen in love everything will work itself out. Later we find that no human intimacy—not even the most satisfying and the most rewarding—can endure without a lot of attention, patience, sacrifice, sensitivity, tenderness and hard work. We also discover that when we are willing to put in such effort, the outcome is extremely rewarding, even if the effort never becomes easy.

Many people have yet to transfer that wisdom about marital intimacy to the parent-child relationship and especially the parent-teenager relationship. The transfer seems especially diffi-

cult for those of us who work with our minds—professionals and
academics. We lack the skills to penetrate into the picture world
of the child or the turbulent, ephemeral world of the teenager.
We lack the patience to work at more than one intimate relationship. Our propensity to reduce everything to ideas and principles
makes us rather poor at the tenderness which even one intimacy
requires. It doesn't seem to be fair that we should have to work
at more than one.

Just as we were tricked by the romantic promise of easy
marital intimacy, we are also tricked by the promise of easy
parenting. All right, kids are a burden when they're little and you
have to feed them and take care of them; but when they have
begun to grow up, ought not it to be enough just to be nice to
them? Why do you have to put in all the extra work of tending
yet another sensitive human intimacy? Why didn't someone
warn us about this?

A few people like my former colleague find the new intimacy
a rewarding challenge and enjoy the wonderful new relationship
that emerges. Most people, however, think that the demands of
intimacy with an adolescent are a pain, a burden, a distraction,
an unfair punishment.

Small wonder that there is so much middle-class alienation
and delinquency.

Some parents do their best and still have trouble. There are
many different factors that go into the development of a teenage
personality and some of them are utterly beyond parental control. Nevertheless, you cannot ignore a young person, or over-
whelm him/her with lectures, or treat her/him as a troublesome
distraction and expect to avoid trouble.

I know of no empirical evidence on how middle-class families cope with the problems of parenting teenagers. I have the
impression, however, from my own experience as a "teenager
priest," that many if not most make a terrible botch of it. They
become concerned only when big problems appear—and by then
it is often too late; much of their concern is devoted to denouncing their kids and blaming them. They are especially quick to
point the finger that accuses the kid of ingratitude: "After all
we've done for you . . ."

Everything indeed has been done, except to listen to what

the child says and to take the child seriously as a person. Parents often seem not to know how to do either of these things and not to want to take the time to learn how.

In *Kramer vs. Kramer* the marriage comes apart because the husband was too busy to listen. One suspects that a lot of marriages are in trouble today for the same reason (though often the wife refuses to listen, too). The same paradigm can be applied to the parent-teenager relationship, except that as the older and more experienced person, the parent is the one who has the first and stronger obligation to listen.

Listening is hard and lecturing is easy. So people give lectures and cheat their kids of the sensitive ear which young people need as they struggle for maturity.

They also cheat themselves of the fun of being a sensitive ear.

The Risks in a Vacation

Vacations are dangerous times for human relationships. Recent psychological research has discovered that for many people, vacations are unhappy and disturbing interludes, mostly because the problems that are implicit in human relationships break into the open and threaten to tear the relationships apart during vacations.

Or to use a more popular description—vacations are times when husbands and wives, parents and children have to put up with one another all day long and discover how much they dislike each other.

The masks and subterfuges, the undiscussed agendas, the careful repression of resentments, frustrations and disappointments don't work quite so well when the normal routine of life, with all its escape hatches, is replaced by the supposedly carefree relaxation of a vacation.

And, worst of all, vacations hold the promise of intimacy, rediscovery and renewal. But however much intimacy may be eagerly anticipated, the reality of intimacy is always terrifying, the threat of rediscovery is frightening, and the possibility of renewal unnerving. Husbands and wives especially quickly turn away from such terrors and seek refuge in fretful bickering and whining self-pity.

Vacations, in other words, are often disastrous precisely because they hold out the possibility of so much happiness, but happiness that must be purchased at the high cost of honesty about all the undiscussed discontent which bogs intimacy down in a swamp of bitterness.

Rarely do we want to pay such costs.

Our intimacies are pasted together by pretense, dishonesty, resentful silences and low-level satisfaction. We settle for such an unhappy compromise because the alternatives seem to be either the end of the intimacy or the paralyzing terror of vulnerability.

If the choice is between vulnerability and a spoiled vacation, most of us will settle for the latter.

And, according to the vacation research, the pretext for spoiling a vacation is guilt—for the working members of the family who feel guilty about leaving the job and for the nonworking members who feel guilty about those members of the family who are left behind.

Guilt about neglected children is a surefire method for destroying a husband/wife vacation in which the threat of renewed love and the disappointment about the failures of such renewal have made the partners intolerable to one another.

Moreover, if you rent a summer place for two weeks, you can easily escape the challenges of more time with those whom you presumably love by permitting your guilt to force you to invite to the house relatives you could see at almost every other time of the year.

That way you can resent the relatives for intruding on your intimacy and resent your partner for not appreciating the relatives enough and resent yourself for somehow "blowing your vacation."

I suppose Neil Simon could write a hilarious comedy about how we deliberately spoil our vacation with guilt, resentment and self-pity.

As a celibate who watches the comedy from a safe distance, I trust I would be excused from laughing at a play about the vacation games families play with each other. I don't find original sin all that funny.

For original sin, finally, is fear, especially the fear of love that says we don't have to fear. A vacation strips away the pretenses under which we hide our fears and reveals how petty and frightened and nasty we can be when another human being threatens to get too close to us and forces us to be attractively vulnerable.

A vacation is that part of the year when we see ourselves clearly the way God sees us all the time: Frightened little children who recoil in horror at the possibility of giving ourselves in trusting love.

It is also that time of the year when married couples perceive more clearly than during the rest of the year how much they hide from one another and how frightened they are at the prospect of taking risks with each other.

So we become guilty about our children or our parents or our siblings or our job. That way we won't feel any guilt about the lost opportunity for love.

Women Will Be Exploited If the Family Deteriorates

Columnist Ellen Goodman recently lamented the apparent decline of the family as reflected in census figures about the diminished size of American households. Maybe, pondered Ms. Goodman, we have mistakenly given up something that was of more value than we realized.

A good deal more analysis will have to be done before the full implications of the census data are understood. Demographic patterns in America are changing. Americans are marrying later, having fewer children and living longer, none of which necessarily means an abandonment of the family. Indeed, you could make a strong case that for most Americans the importance of the family as a source of fundamental life satisfaction is greater than it has ever been before.

Yet Ms. Goodman's concern about the family is both appropriate and interesting. Unlike a substantial number of ideological feminists, she does think the family is essential to the rights of women. She is not in the camp, for example, of some women graduate students in archeology who accuse male paleoanthropologists of anti-woman chauvinism because they think familial predispositions have been coded into our genes by the evolutionary process (a strange complaint, because the paleoanthropological evolutionary perspective can be used to make a powerful case for the equality of men and women).

Why such young women scholars think the family is a threat to a woman's plight is hard to understand. Historically and sociologically, the family is much more likely to protect women than to imprison them, though certain family structures make things hard on women—including the middle-class liberal feminist American family structure, which demands that men be good at doing men's things and women be good at doing both women's and men's things.

Historically, it has been very difficult to maintain civilization when family ties decline. The family, even at its most oppressive, offers a place in the social structure where the human person may fit. It is the last barrier against anonymity, isolation, loneliness and despair. Deprive humans of a family to which to belong and the ties binding the social structure together will fray, loosen and break. If the social structure collapses, civilization evanesces and the jungle returns. Nor is it the jungle of our prehominid, hunter-gatherer ancestors who were bound together with tight community ties; rather, it is the jungle of the modern urban metropolis in which the individual is worth only the price he or she brings in the open marketplace.

The feminist assault on the family is mindless madness; it is only in civilization that there can be discussion of the rights of women. In an anonymous, alienated, dangerous jungle, women are prey: Used, battered and exploited by those creatures who are physically stronger than they. Whoever attacks family attacks civilization, and whoever attacks civilization puts women in grave danger. The career woman who is lonely, isolated, detached, seemingly self-sufficient is, in fact, a perfect target, the ideal victim in the modern urban jungle.

Not every woman has to have a family, needs to have a family, should have a family. But if family life deteriorates, the freedom and dignity of women are in jeopardy. The wise woman begins to take karate lessons.

Religion and
Sex Are Inseparable

For most eras of human history, religion and sex have been inseparable. Most humans who have ever lived would find the apparent opposition between the two in our day—most notably exemplified by the anti-sex, anti-woman attitudes expressed at the Synod of Bishops in Rome last fall—to be utterly incomprehensible. Both sex and religion deal with life, the continuation of life, the persistence of life, the indestructibility of life. Sex was a religious phenomenon, and religion was profoundly concerned about sexuality.

The fertility ritual was the religious rite par excellence. All three of the symbols, for example, in the Jewish Passover and the Christian Easter—the Paschal Lamb, the unleavened bread and the mixing of fire and water—are fertility rituals, representing the explosion of new life in the springtime; the fire and water imagery, somewhat vague in the Jewish Passover story but vivid in the Christian Easter liturgy, quite explicitly represents the mingling of the male (fire) and the female (water) as a source of new life. The words as the candle is plunged into the water, "May this flame fructify these waters," leaves no doubt about what the early Christian liturgists had in mind when they took over the Roman pagan fire and water fertility rite.

Moreover, in the ordinary lives of everyday human beings,

there persist powerful correlations between vivid religious imagery and intense religious devotion on the one hand and sexual fulfillment and marriage on the other. In one recent study of young adults, in only about one third of the marriages did both husband and wife say that their sexual fulfillment was excellent. When both husband and wife had strong positive religious images and where both prayed every day, then three quarters said the sexual fulfillment was excellent. Moreover, this particular study focused on marriages in which at least one partner was Catholic. In other words, despite the negativism of Catholic sexual teaching, ordinary married people are able to relate intense religion to intense intimacy.

Careful studies of this relationship are to be found in a new book called *Marital Intimacy: A Catholic Perspective*, by a woman psychiatrist and a woman theologian (Joan Anzia and Mary Durkin), published by Andrews and McMeel, Inc. By the very fact that both of these authors are married women and mothers, they are disqualified by the Catholic hierarchy from knowing anything that is of any importance about marriage. Nonetheless, their study of how religion and sexuality relate to one another at critical stages in the marriage cycle—falling in love, settling down, bottoming out, beginning again—is an innovative and powerful commentary on the Catholic experience of marriage (and I must overcome some sibling rivalry to say that). The hierarchy will not listen, of course, because the hierarchy already knows all the answers and even if it didn't it would be unable to turn to women for insights.

It is in this context of the "natural" relationship between religion and sex that I defend myself against all the outraged protests against my recent column about how translators have watered down the sexual imagery of the Bible and particularly of the Song of Solomon. One writer, however, pointed out quite correctly that there is an excellent translation of the Song of Solomon in the *Good News Bible* published by the American Bible Society. Thus: "How beautiful are your feet in sandals. The curve of your thighs is like the work of an artist. A bowl is there that never runs out of spiced wine. A sheaf of wheat is there surrounded by lilies. Your breasts are like twin deer . . . your neck is like a tower of ivory . . . your head is held high like Mt.

Carmel . . . your braided hair shines like the finest satin." The translator did a nifty job. He was able to convey the meaning of the text and in a sufficiently delicate way that it could be printed in a general newspaper. But there was one problem he couldn't solve even with his skill and delicacy: How do you tell the reader that when the girl says to her lover that he is as firm and as upright as Mt. Lebanon, it is not his backbone that she has in mind?

The two young people in the Song are hopelessly in love with one another. Presumably they passed out of that phase as time went on. Drs. Durkin and Anzia argue, however, that the rebirth of romance is a natural and healthy part of the marriage cycle and that the principal function of religion is to provide the motives and the vision for the rebirth of romantic love that confirms the marriage bond through the ups and downs of time.

Obviously an idea which the Catholic bishops and all other prudes and puritans could not possibly accept.

Why Teens Become Pregnant

One out of every ten teenage women will be pregnant before their twentieth birthday, most of them out of wedlock. Those who have sowed the wind of permissiveness are now appalled to be reaping the teenage pregnancy (and herpes epidemic) whirlwind.

A standard response to the alarming increase in pregnancy among teens is to attribute it to the absence of adequate birth control information. Provide teenage girls with birth control information and techniques, argues this conventional wisdom, and the problem will go away.

Thus do humans respond when, having abandoned wisdom —and even belief in the possibility of wisdom—and not yet acquired a sophisticated understanding of behavior, they turn to fad and fashion, to cliché and stereotype, for solutions to pressing and poignant problems.

There is ample evidence that many if not most teen pregnancies are at least partially intended—more so perhaps in some subcultures than in others. If a young woman in her late teens, the high point of her fertility, wants to have a child, consciously or unconsciously or in some mixture of the two, the odds are excellent that she will.

Teenagers like to have babies. Their bodies are ready for childbearing, their minds are fascinated by the prospect, their curiosity about motherhood is enormous. When circumstances permit, many teenagers will bear children—not all teenagers of course, but many. Or to put the matter more precisely, there is a powerful propensity in the body and the personality of most teenage girls toward motherhood, not an irresistible propensity certainly and not one that ought to be encouraged surely—but still one that must be taken very seriously.

For a long time the human race's survival depended on young women beginning to bear children almost as soon as they could. Those who were especially inclined to do so were more likely to make their contribution to the subsequent gene pool. It is no accident that the years of highest fertility immediately follow sexual maturation. In the history of the human species the best chances for reproduction had to be while a woman was most likely to be alive. Surviving to childbearing age was a major accomplishment for a girl child; she must then make her contribution to the continuation of the race (or the transmission of her own genes, depending on your biological model) in the few years of life which were still left to her.

The evolutionary motivation for early childbearing is not the determining of human behavior. It is not a biological necessity, nor even one whose resistance is "unnatural" or harmful. Indeed, in a society like ours, where the cultural responsibilities of motherhood are so enormous, a teenage girl is unlikely to be prepared for the bearing of a child.

The point to be remembered, however, is that even though the survival of the race and the transmission of one's own genes no longer depend on teenage pregnancies, there is a dimension of a young woman's personality, bequested to her from our evolutionary past, which does not quite comprehend this recent and dramatic change. Her intellect may grasp the point, her body does not understand it fully.

Furthermore, psychologically speaking, producing a baby is

something a teenage girl can do. If she feels worthless or un-wanted, or useless or confused, having a child is an excellent way of asserting her womanly worth—as well as punishing or screaming for help to those who do not notice her or put too much pressure on her or do not seem to love her.

It has always been hard to grow up, and probably harder for women than for men, because parenting is harder for women than for men. Delayed social maturation—adolescence—may be essential in our society, but it makes growing up more difficult, again, one suspects, especially for young women. In our times most especially, when there is so much confusion and uncer-tainty about the proper role of women—young women find that they must be both women and men—it is not at all surprising that teenage girls flee from the burdens of such confusion by as-serting their primal womanliness.

I'm often asked if teenagers have changed in the last cen-tury. My response is that they have not changed much, but they seem much more fragile today, much more uncertain, much more easily hurt. I would add that this is especially true of young women.

So why teenage pregnancies? Permissiveness? Sure. Igno-rance? Partially. Powerful biological propensities, rooted in our evolutionary past? Undoubtedly. But fragility, the need to be loved, fear of one's own worthlessness? If you leave that out, you miss the most important fact of all.

And you don't cure that last problem by making sure your teenage girl has a packet of birth control pills in her purse.

Civilizing the Ape

How do humans learn to think of sex objects as persons?

Rape, sexual harassment in the work place (reported by 40 percent of female federal employees), exploitation, manipulation —all occur because the object of sexual desire ceases to become a person and becomes a thing. Even in marriage the other is frequently a sex object and not a person. The pope was quite right recently (if misunderstood because of horrendous press relations) when he said that degradation is as bad as adultery.

Why do human beings do such things to one another?

How do they learn, if ever, to stop doing them? The "sexual objectification" of women by men is a paradigm of such dehumanization and depersonalization. Women do it to men, too, if in a far more subtle way.

Recently, I was in an airport in a medium-sized Midwestern city waiting for an airplane near a group of college athletes. My clerical identification sufficiently obscured, these healthy young apes did not notice me. A stewardess walked through the lounge out onto the ramp and up to the plane. The apes' discussion of her was clinical, gross and crude, and their shared fantasy of what they would like to do to her, harsh and brutal.

Mind you, they did not harass her personally. She did not hear what they were saying. Although in this day and age young college men do not do such things in airports, their locker-room attitude toward her was the same that one could have heard thirty years ago. They would not assault her, of course, partly because of social controls and partly because of internalized values. If the controls should disappear and the values collapse, some of those young men would assault attractive women if there was not cost to them in doing so.

I wondered whether such "locker-room" mentality is a biological inevitability in the human male animal, or is it, perhaps, a mixture of culture and biology that could be eliminated only with enormous difficulty from the human species? Is it inevitable that young human males go through an ape stage in which a woman is only or mostly an object of pleasure?

It is unfair to compare such locker-room rapists with apes, for apes are not cruel or brutal to their sexual partners. The cruelty of dehumanizing another person into a pleasure object is uniquely human.

Several days later on television there were interviews with two somewhat older and considerably fiercer apes—defensive halfbacks of the Chicago Bears who had just become fathers. (The defensive team of the Chicago Bears is, indeed, fierce. The offensive team remains better undiscussed.) Both young men had assisted at the births of their daughters, and both discussed the meaning of the experience to them with tenderness and sensitivity that was quite moving. The women in their lives—wife and daughter, both—were not objects, but persons. I wondered if five or six years ago their attitudes may have been no different from the younger apes I had heard in the airport. Had the experience of marriage and paternity humanized the ape?

Perhaps the pertinent question is not whether the human animal can be prevented from going through a phase in life in which he/she objectifies persons of the other sex. Perhaps, the question is how that stage can be transcended, and how we can be prevented from either fixating at or slipping back into the locker-room phase of our lives. The frequency of sexual harassment in the work place suggests that a lot of us never develop beyond the locker-room stage.

An intimate relationship with a person of the opposite sex clearly makes a major contribution to such a development. But there has to be some capacity or respectful intimacy from childhood to begin with, or any close relationship will deteriorate into exploitation. Judging from the enormous amount of sexual depersonalization in our society, we have a long way to go in the art of raising adults who are not sexual brutes.

The Irish and Sex

It being so close to St. Patrick's Day, it's time to set the record straight on the Irish—a lost cause if there ever was one. The part of the record we propose to set straight today is the reputation the Irish have for being sexual puritans, a reputation that the Irish themselves do all they can to confirm.

Despite the color of their home country, the Irish and the Irish Americans have always believed that the grass is greener in someone else's yard. Other peoples, they argue, must be having more fun with sex than we do.

'Tis not true as far as the empirical evidence goes, but if you're Irish the last thing in the world you want to lose on St.

Patrick's Day—or any other day for that matter—is your self-pity.

In fact, the Irish tradition of literature and law is probably the most erotic in Europe and certainly the most feminist. Pope Adrian IV gave Ireland to his fellow Englishman King John so that the king would clean up the sexual mess among the Irish clergy and laity. (Even in those days the popes acted as if they had more power than they really possessed.) King John wasn't very successful at the task, but after a half-millennium or so the English finally managed to turn the Irish into puritans like themselves.

It took genocide to do it, though the English have never been known to hesitate about such things when it suits the cause of their imperial power.

As late as the synod of Maynooth in 1450, the Irish lords (lay and spiritual) considered an item condemning the exercise of the rights of the old Brehon laws—polygamy, trial marriages of a year and a day, women instigating divorce and suchlike. No vote was taken on the item because virtually all of the lords present were still following the Brehon customs.

Moreover, the old Irish wake involved not only drinking in the room with the corpse, but making love in the fields around the deceased's house, a kind of thumbing of the nose at death. It was a pagan custom that the church never liked, as one might imagine. The wake has been cleaned up in America and eliminated in Ireland, yet the combination of death and sex lurks just beneath the surface of the Irish heritage and what the scholars call the "grotesque" in Irish humor and literature.

Pagan or not, defying death with sex is an assertion that the forces of life are stronger than the forces of death. The Irish have believed that in both their pagan and Christian manifestations.

There is a puritanical side to the Irish heritage, but it coexists with a sensuous and even licentious aspect of the heritage. The Irish culture is dualistic, oscillating between sensuality and penitence as in the wonderful O'Faillon short story about the middle-aged lovers who crawl up Cro Patrick together and then go back to their hotel in Salt Hill and celebrate their virtue with a night of love.

Since 1850 the puritanical side of the Irish may have dominated. Late marriage and sexual repression, however, were not natural to the culture. Rather, they were the results of the devastating blow of the Great Famine which killed half the population, while the English smugly watched and shipped food out of the country instead of into it. The Irish married late because they could not afford to marry young and raise large families. The church opposed late marriages instead of supporting them, precisely because it feared sexual repression involved in such delays. Eventually the church too was swallowed up by the grim, life-denying effects of the famine genocide.

Any discussion of the puritanical strain of the Irish personality and the power of that strain in the last hundred years that does not take into account the oppression of five centuries and the effects of the famine is intellectually dishonest and bigoted.

The Irish are now prospering in the Common Market and the American Irish are more than prospering in the New World. The effects of the famine are finally wearing off. The rest of the world better beware.

So on St. Patrick's Day the Irish continue to tell death what it can do. Any culture that can say that deserves to dye rivers green, paint streets green and generally create disturbances once a year . . . on the feast of a saint who wasn't even Irish.

Sex and Suicide
Linked Among Teens?

All summer the national media have told us about the increase in teenage sex and teenage suicide. No one seems to have raised the obvious question: If both promiscuity and suicide rates are going up among teenagers, are the two problems linked? Does an environment in which promiscuity is taken for granted, even considered virtuous, lead to more self-destruction?

There's not much doubt that the two increases are related to one another; however, the correlation is what social scientists call "spurious"—an apparent relationship between two phenomena that is in fact the result of a connection between both of them and some prior phenomenon. Promiscuity and suicide are both forms of self-destruction that result from a more basic difficulty.

There are a lot of names for it—loneliness, self-hatred, low self-esteem, lack of self-respect. The best label though is self-contempt. Teens do themselves in one way or another because they have contempt for themselves. "Permissiveness" or the "new morality" celebrated in the *Newsweek* article on teenage sex is the result, not the cause, of self-contempt.

The body is the person. You give your personhood recklessly to others or demand that others give their bodies recklessly to you because you don't think your body and your person are worth very much. The new morality may be partly a rationalization of hedonism, but it is much more an excuse for self-contempt. You can punish and destroy yourself while all the while you prate about how modern and open and free you are.

Young people are caught in two binds. Much of our morality was shaped in an era when sex had as one of its primary purposes the assurance that family property would be transmitted to members of one's own clan. You paid a bride price to your wife's father for her virginity to assure that someone else's child would not inherit your family possessions. However, mixed in with these economic motivations were insights and wisdom about the nature of human nature. Chastity may no longer be an economic necessity; it does not follow, however, that it is no longer a dimension of self-respect. Moral and psychological teachers have not done their homework in separating wisdom from economics; hence adolescents must face the problems of maturation—without any clear and persuasive wisdom about how you respect yourself and others in sexual encounters.

Moreover, our species is biologically engineered to begin reproduction early. For most of our history as primates, reproduction had to start in the teens (as it still does among the primitive hunter-gatherers) because life was so short and infant and maternal mortality rates were so high. Our primate nature causes our reproductive capabilities and energies to be strongest in the teen years. However, our nature as a primate who loves requires us to achieve emotional maturity before we enter into a more or less permanent, more or less pair-bonded relationship with a member of the opposite sex.

To make matters worse for contemporary adolescents, they mature earlier physically (and probably have stronger sexual energies) because of better diet and better health care, but mature much later emotionally because of the long period of education (and economic dependence) required to emerge as a self-financing adult in our society. A whole decade may intervene between the time when the reproductive energies are at their peak and marriage, and there is no clear wisdom about how to cope with those years.

Hence, sex becomes a superb way to mess yourself up. You can also do drugs, or drink, or commit suicide, too. Or you can combine them all. One can't sell chastity as a form of self-respect to kids who think they merit no respect. To paraphrase the old dictum about labor law, "Hell for kids, purgatory for parents, and heaven for psychotherapists."

Why the self-contempt? The answer to that is easy: Even though we claim to be a child-centered society, we have contempt for our kids, particularly for our teenage kids. They are loud, noisy, obnoxious, and unmotivated, it seems, to the performance which will guarantee success for them and acclaim for us who are responsible for them. If adults—parents, teachers, clergy, police—have contempt for young people, we ought not to be surprised that the kids have contempt for themselves.

We may do a lot of things for our children, but "doing a lot" isn't the same as loving them, especially when we "do" many of the things secretly, resenting the drain on our time, energy and money. "Sacrificing" for the kids is often a mask for disliking them. They see through the mask. As the Irish put it, "If you love your kids too much, it will spoil them and they won't work." You can love teenagers the wrong way perhaps, but you can't love them too much. Self-contempt is an epidemic disease among adolescents, because love from their relevant adults is far more rare than some of the surveys suggest physical virginity is. Why respect yourself when no one else respects you?

Fearing Sex

The Hite Report on Male Sexuality offers an interesting challenge to organized religion, one that religion will very likely ignore.

As objective scholarship, Ms. Hite's book is not worth the paper it is written on. Her sampling technique is of the same sort that enabled the *Literary Digest* to predict that Alfred M. Landon would defeat Franklin Roosevelt in the 1936 presidential election. As prose, Ms. Hite's literary style is turgid and dull; as an objective and sensitive discussion of human sexuality, the book does not even begin to explain, so twisted and maimed is it by her radical and hate-filled feminist ideology.

Nonetheless, *The Hite Report* makes one enormously important point which, if it is not new, at least needs to be repeated again and again and again: Men are as afraid of sex as women, and as frustrated and disappointed in their sexual activity.

The fear of sex, the flight from sex, the experience of a deterioration of sexual payoff in the relatively early stages of sustained intimacy—these are not men's problems or women's problems. They are human problems. Moreover, they are profoundly religious problems because they touch inevitably on fundamental questions about the nature of the self and the purpose and destiny of human life.

A man and a woman turn away from their initial passionate attraction to one another precisely because they lose their nerve; they lose their nerve because they lack the confidence in the worth and dignity of their own personhood and in the purpose and graciousness of human life. The fears and frustrations, the timidities and the terrors, the anxiety and the fractured dreams of human intimacy are, in the final analysis, not problems of sexuality, but problems of religion. You can risk yourself in the terrors of human intimacy only if you are convinced that you are worth loving; you can continue that risk, despite suffering and heartache, only if you are convinced that ultimately life is worth living. Men and women are afraid of sex because they do not think they are worth loving and life is worth living—not, at any rate, when one risks rejection, resentment and ridicule.

The Vatican periodically warns Catholic married people about the dangers of "unbridled passion." As one of my married colleagues remarked, "Don't they realize that the real danger for married people is bridled passion? That our problems would indeed be solved if we had a little more unbridled passion?"

Unfortunately, the conservative traditions are busy defending all the negative sexual prohibitions from the past and the liberal denominations are busy telling people that it's all right to do the things they were once forbidden to do. On neither side of the denominational divide does there seem to be any awareness that for reasons of logistics, if nothing else, most sex is between married people who will not divorce one another and who are more or less faithful to each other. For such folks the problem is neither keeping the old rules nor breaking them. It is, rather, keeping the intensity of love alive despite the monotony and routine of daily life, the silence engendered by community and family, the cynicism that comes from giving up hope, and the anger that results from broken dreams.

Are not monotony, anger, cynicism and fear precisely the human weaknesses that religion is supposed to exorcise? Are not these demons that upset human sexual intimacy the enemies from which religion purports to free us? When such demons destroy human passions, the churches are strangely silent.

The religious right will denounce *The Hite Report*, the religious left will defend it, and neither will understand the poignant appeal that it presents to religious vision.

John Gagnon, a sociologist who has studied American sexual life with great professional competence, recently wrote, "How can sex with the same partner be boring when tennis isn't? Perhaps it's all tactics and practice . . ."

And motivation. As any tennis player knows, a doubles team is as good as the motivation of both its members. Religion cannot provide lovers with a detailed catalog of tactics, and it certainly cannot command them to practice. It can, however, provide them with the motivation for love and the courage which love requires.

Love and courage, that's what religion is.

PRIESTHOOD

Most priests hate my guts.

And mostly because I dare to say the unsayable: Sunday homilies are lousy.

You can criticize the pope, the bishops, the Curia, the administration, the educational system, the media, anything you want. And it doesn't bother priests at all.

But don't dare criticize them.

Don't suggest that it is hypocritical for the National Federation of Priests' Councils to denounce injustice around the world and ignore the injustice of poor preaching.

The laity pays our salaries to preach the Word. And they have a right in strict justice to good preaching. Failure to preach effectively is a violation of justice which demands restitution.

But neither the NFPC nor its member bodies give a damn about the professional performance of the priest in the pulpit.

And every time I write a column in which I say that four fifths of the laity gives us bad marks on our preaching even though the empirical data show that the quality of preaching is the most important predictor of identification with the church, another Catholic paper or two, yielding to clerical pressure, drops the column.

Peter Garrity, the reputedly liberal archbishop of Newark, even canceled me in a Jove from Olympus editorial on the front page of the Newark Advocate.

So much for freedom of expression and liberalism in Newark.

I don't care. Homilies are still terrible. The clergy needs to be told that repeatedly.

The laity knows it already.

Reflections on the Priesthood

I've been a priest for twenty-seven years now. No one warned me about either the advantages or the disadvantages on that chilly day in May 1954. Oh, they warned me about the obvious problems and the obvious payoffs, but those turn out to be less important than the unexpected pleasures and punishments.

More than for most men, for example, it is tolerable for priests to display sensitivity, tenderness, compassion. The fierce competitiveness of the male occupational world—made even worse these days by women who want to compete—deprives most men of any opportunity to develop the "softer" part of their personalities. They must be tough, hard-nosed, macho competitors and cannot even permit themselves much in the way of authentic friendship. A lot of priests are the same way, of course, but we don't have to be that way and if we're not no one thinks that somehow we're less than completely male—though some men do look down on us because we don't have to "prove" our maleness in the "real" world of jungle competition.

Priests are also able to have close relationships with women because their celibate commitment makes them a "safe" friend (though not as safe as formerly) and a friend who will be understanding and sympathetic. Most other men are terrified of such relationships—even with their wives.

Moreover, kids like us. If you make a funny face at a little kid while you're wearing the Roman collar, the tyke will giggle back at you and you've won a friend. You are an ambassador from the world of adults who is utterly acceptable when you enter the world of children. Just try doing that when you don't have the collar on.

Finally, you are the important one at critical turning points. As one of my students put it, the whole point in having clergypersons is that they "exist"; you may not want to pay attention to them a good deal of the time, but the fact that they are there to turn to when you need them makes them the most important people in the world. In the current perspective, a clergyperson is supposed to have problems just like everyone else and at the same time be better able (because of his/her faith) to cope with such problems and hence be a model for others. Impossible? Sure, but not unimportant.

On the other hand, if you try anything else while remaining a priest, your priesthood will be held against you. Editors, especially Catholic editors, will insist that you shouldn't write a column because church and journalism should be as separate as church and state. Sociologists will say that you can't be a priest and a good scholar. Writers and book reviewers will be incensed if you should write a novel (especially if, like my book—which was published on my anniversary in the priesthood—it looks as if it's going to be popular). If you are successful in any of these extra areas, church authorities will go after you on the premise that any priest who writes for a lot of people must be bad.

On the right, they will say that by telling the truth about the church (in social science, journalism or fiction) you are causing grave harm to the "faithful" (who the "faithful" are is never precisely specified); on the left, they will envy you, psychoanalyze you, even—as did one left-wing Catholic writer recently—publish long essays about the clothes you wear (not impeded by the truth, incidentally). Both the right and the left will try to punish your relatives for their crime of being related to you.

I'm not complaining. The pluses are more than the minuses. I'd do it all again. But I must tell those who are joining the ranks of the priesthood this year to be wary of those who say that the church and their fellow priests will stand by them and support them.

They lie. The church tries to destroy its priests, and the worst enemies that a priest has are his fellow priests.

"Casting Fire"
Is Mark of a Good Priest

If you have a priest who doesn't disconcert you, then maybe you should ask yourself what kind of priest he is. The priest, especially the celibate priest, is the hint of another world, a world beyond this one, dumped down into the middle of human life; his mission is to shake people up, not by screaming or shouting at them, but by reminding them that the conventional wisdom about human life is very probably wrong.

People are fascinated by priests and are, I find, fascinated by novels about priests, especially when such novels are written by priests. I asked my editor why. Her response was illuminating: "Priests are terribly intriguing people. Everyone wonders why a man would live the way a priest does, and they're a little frightened by the reality he seems to see a little more clearly than they do."

A woman who has been a very close friend of mine for a long time became very angry at me recently. "Now is the time in your life when you should settle down and enjoy the benefits from all the work you've done. Instead, you seem to go around looking for things to do that will get you in more trouble. Why do you have to write novels? You are only going to cause heartache for you and those who love you."

She had not read the book in question and I gather (since she no longer speaks to me) that she still has not read it. It was not the content of the book that upset her but the fact that I was embarking on a new adventure which would certainly make trouble. Why couldn't I settle down and act sensibly for a change? Why not become a respectable, proper, uncontroversial Catholic clergyman?

I understand the concern and the affection that went into

the question. Yet in fact she was saying, "Why don't you stop being a priest?" But by very definition, a priest is someone who can never settle down and be respectable. He must always be stirring up the pot, adding fuel to the fire, making trouble, precisely because he follows in the footsteps of one who said that he came to cast fire on the earth.

You obviously don't have to write novels to cast fire on the earth, but whenever a clergyman thinks that he has now done enough and can settle back and fit in nicely with others, then he's in deep trouble as a clergyman. It is his role to endlessly stand for new possibilities, renewed hope, rekindled enthusiasm, dreams that young men shall dream and dreams that old men shall see. A priest must be perennially young in dreaming dreams for others and perpetually old in seeing visions for others.

For Catholics, there is considerable difficulty in coping with the changing role of the priest as he comes out of the rectory and into the mainstream of society, perhaps for the first time in the last half-millennium. To tell you the truth, the priest does not "fit"; he is an odd man out, and not merely as an extra person at a dinner party. It's all right for a priest to be disconcerting when he stays in the rectory and does not enter into close relationships with other human beings, for then he is not really disconcerting. He's an odd man out, but far enough out so as not to be a threat. When he is an odd man in, in your family, at your dinner, in your friendship group, then he is one very disconcerting person to have around.

Many of the Catholic laity, it seems to me, appear delighted to have "lap dog" priests around, clergymen you can pat on the head and patronize, but the last person in the world they really want a close friendship with is a priest who will constantly remind them of the one who came to cast fire on the earth.

Encouragement Can Reverse
the Shortage of New Priests

The shortage of priests in the Catholic Church is going to get much worse. The impact of resignations and the decline in recruitment of priests is only now beginning to be felt. But as careful research, directed by Richard Schoenherr of the University of Wisconsin, demonstrates, the next ten years are going to see a drastic decline in the number of priests available to American Catholics.

In 1969 there were over 900 priests ordained in the United States. In 1991, according to the Wisconsin projection, there will only be 229 ordained. There were 40,000 priests in the late 1960s. By the early 1990s there will be, even in the most promising scenario, no more than 25,000.

The Wisconsin team does not attempt to explain the reason why young men are so much less likely to want to be priests. Many Catholics assume that the reason is either that the priesthood does not have the prestige it used to have or that Catholic parents are not as proud of having a priest in their family as they used to be, or that young men are not as willing as they once were to commit themselves to a life of celibacy.

These reasons, however, do not seem to stand up in the face of research that my colleagues and I at the National Opinion Research Center conducted. Young Catholics still admire and respect priests. Half the Catholic adults in the country still say they would be proud to have a son who is a priest. And most young men going to the seminary now realize that whatever the legal restrictions may be, it is socially quite acceptable to leave the priesthood after a period of service.

Our evidence suggests that the principal factor in the decline of priestly vocations is the absence of encouragement that young men inclined toward the priesthood used to receive, especially encouragement from the two most important sources—the parish priest and the mother.

Priests no longer seem very enthusiastic about recruiting young men to take their places. The identity crisis and the loss of nerve that has affected American Catholic priests for the last decade seem to have drained their energies and destroyed their zeal for recruiting other men to be priests.

Mothers hesitate to encourage their sons to be priests, both because the much-publicized resignations of unhappy priests make mothers wonder whether happiness and the priesthood are compatible, and because mothers are acutely conscious of the loneliness of old age (in part because many of them are trying to tend to their lonely parents) and the apparent special loneliness of elderly priests. "They have no family to take care of them," one woman told me sadly.

There are many solutions proposed for the coming shortage of priests, most notably the ordination of women and permission for married priests to return to the ministry. I support the former and also with some reservations the latter, but our research shows that relatively few young women are that interested in becoming priests and that perhaps only one out of ten resigned priests would return to the full-time ministry if they could do so and remain married. Moreover, our research shows that while celibacy makes men hesitate about becoming priests (it doubtless always has), it is no more an important factor in impending vocations than is the decline of encouragement from priests and from mothers.

Therefore, the path for church leadership is reasonably clear. Restore the self-confidence of priests and reassure mothers and you will start getting young men in the seminaries again. In fact, these two relatively simple strategies are not likely to be followed. Bishops, as well as their fellow priests, are almost criminally fatalistic about the decline in vocations, accepting it (sometimes, one thinks, almost joyously) as a necessary, inevitable phenomenon.

It is not. The decline in seminary enrollments can be reversed, but only by men of faith and courage and vision. There are not enough such men either in the presbyterate or the hierarchy, and that is the real problem.

On Bad Sermons

The greatest single problem facing the American Catholic Church is not papal authority or sex or consumerism. Rather, the most serious threat to Catholicism is to be found in the mediocrity and immaturity of its clergy.

Consider the facts: The quality of Sunday preaching is four times more important in the identification of Catholics with their church than are birth control, divorce, abortion, papal authority and the ordination of women put together. Yet, in the mid-1970s, 20 percent of the American Catholics thought the Sunday preaching they heard was excellent—as opposed to almost 50 percent the decade before. By the end of the 1970s, for Catholics under thirty, the proportion went down to 10 percent. The most important thing that priests do they do very badly indeed.

Moreover, even though these facts are now well known, Catholic clergy in the United States have not been able to muster a response to them. At a recent meeting of the National Federation of Priests' Councils—the professional association of the Catholic clergy—a presentation based on the phenomenon that the laity gives the clergy very low ratings both on the quality of their preaching and the quality of their pastoral ministry stirred no reaction at all from the elected representatives of the priests of the country. They were much more interested in discussing missionary involvement in politics in Latin America. As one priest remarked, "We are responsible for the whole world, not just for our parish," doubtless an excellent reason for ignoring the collective failure of the clergy in their parishes. At the end of the meeting, the assembled delegates voted enthusiastically to support missionary involvement in political activities in foreign countries and to demand gun control. There was nary a word of self-censure, however, for the failure of the clergy to honor their obligation to preach a good Sunday sermon or the delegates to address themselves to such massive professional failure.

It is unthinkable that any other professional organization, when faced with the evidence of its own incompetence, would totally ignore the problem. Only the most immature personalities could react in such a fashion. Justice for the Third World, indeed, but not justice for the Sunday congregation.

Nor can it be argued that the National Federation of Priests' Councils is unrepresentative of this country's clergy. None of the individual priests' senates and organizations around the nation have reacted any differently, and there is no evidence of developing crash programs by which priests might upgrade the awesome mediocrity of their preaching.

There was a time when the obscurity of Latin and the doctrine of a sacramental service that worked independently of the virtue of the one who administered the sacrament enabled the Catholics to take their preaching responsibilities much less seriously than their Protestant counterparts. After all, Catholics had to come to church on Sunday regardless of the quality of the sermons and Protestants did not. So why worry about the quality of preaching? The National Federation of Priests' Councils and the priest leadership in the country are apparently well aware of all the other changes in the church, but they have yet to comprehend the fact that the laity no longer feels that they have to go to church on Sunday and that the quality of preaching for Catholics is at least as important as it is for Protestants. One is forced to conclude that the clerical leadership has not noticed this change because it does not want to.

The mediocrity and immaturity of the Catholic clergy is reinforced by the extremely powerful informal social controls maintained within the priesthood—far more powerful, in fact, than the formal controls exercised over priests by bishops and by higher levels in the church. Any Catholic clergyman who rises above the level of common mediocrity is immediately sanctioned by an enormously powerful and extremely effective system of envy that assails not only him but his family and his friends. Skill, to say nothing of excellence, is absolutely intolerable in clerical cultures, perhaps because the reward system for Catholic priests is so limited and those who do anything exceptionally well are perceived as unlikely to be rewarded.

There are, of course, many mature and competent Catholic

priests in the United States, but as a collectivity, the Catholic presbyterate is characterized by neither quality.

The only hope for change will come from the laity that picks up, including indirectly, the tab for the priest delegates to go off to a luxury hotel for several days of meaningless blather. The mediocrity of the Roman clergy, it is to be feared, will change only when the laity decrees that he who does not preach will not be paid.

Problems of the Priesthood—I

This is the first in a series of columns on problems in the priesthood. I want to make clear at the beginning that I do not intend this series to be a series of generalizations that apply to all priests or to any specific priest. Rather, they are a set of observations about propensities and behavior patterns that are part of clerical culture, and unless and until the responsible parties of the church—bishops and heads of priests' associations, I presume—are prepared to deal with these problems, the morale and the effectiveness of the presbyterate will continue to diminish.

The first of the critical problems facing the priesthood is the absence of loyalty in the presbyterate. We heard much in the seminary about the "great fraternity" of priests. Priests, we were told, stood by one another. Priests were generous and kind to one another. Priests helped one another. Priests rejoiced in one another's successes and sorrowed for one another's failures. Priests rushed to one another's aid with enthusiastic support, and when they were attacked they stood by one another.

I will confess that I, perhaps more naive than most, believed that stuff, not only in the seminary but for about the first decade of my life in the priesthood. Then I discovered to my dismay that we had been lied to, that priests aren't that way at all. What passes for fraternity is in fact a rigid and vicious system of social control that strives to level everyone at the lowest common denominator of mediocrity. What appears to be support is really stern control mixed with a vigilant watchfulness to see that no priest does anything that might gain him any attention.

I suppose I should have guessed that this was the way things really were, even in the seminary, when I heard the Jesuit faculty at my seminary patronizing the late great John Courtney Murray. It was very subtle, though: They seemed to be praising Murray, but there was a little twist at the end, usually something like, "John is so difficult to read that nobody's really quite sure what he's up to. Sometimes we think not even John himself."

I do not want to single out the Jesuits for special reproach. If their patronizing was so offensive, the only reason was that they had more talented and well-trained priests of whom to be proud; the Jesuits' "star system" in those days always guaranteed a certain amount of lavish praise for the designated stars, who usually were the second-raters and not the first. In the diocesan priesthood, there was not and is not praise for anyone, no honest positive evaluation of work, no defense of a priest under attack, no praise for a priest who does well, no enthusiasm for a priest who is popular, no defense of a priest who is defamed.

Quite the contrary. The clerical-culture rumor network always has the "inside story" about Teilhard de Chardin's mistress, or Cardinal Suenen's unpopularity with his own priests, or Bishop Sheen's dramatic gestures, or John Murray's obscurities, or Hans Küng's pride (all of which stories I am prepared to testify are simply false). Sometimes, indeed, it would appear that priests will stop at absolutely nothing to defame, punish, hurt and, if possible, destroy one of their own when anyone seems to be remarkable.

There is precious little loyalty in the priesthood. The great fraternity was a noble idea. It also is virtually essential for an effectively performing presbyterate. The only trouble with the great fraternity is that in the real world it is a fraternity of envy and little else.

Problems of
the Priesthood—II

Arrogance is one of the abiding problems of the presbyterate. I use the word in a very specific sense: There is a powerful temptation in the presbyterate to believe that because one is a priest, what one says or thinks is important regardless of whether one has any special knowledge or any professional competence on which to base one's judgments.

I have been inundated with letters from priests denouncing *The Cardinal Sins*, while cheerfully admitting that they have not read the book. Lots of people express opinions about books they haven't read. But only priests are sufficiently arrogant to admit that they haven't read a book and still assume that they can get away with saying what they think about it.

As I said when I began this series on problems in the presbyterate, I do not claim that all priests or even a majority of priests act this way. My point is that the propensity to pontificate though ignorant seems to be built into the structure of clerical culture. A lot of people act that way and the rest of us are at least tempted often to behave as though we knew everything about everything.

Thus, we have the Synod of Bishops assembling in Rome, which, innocent of any input from married couples, is laying down all kinds of rules and regulations about the nature of marriage and family life. The National Federation of Priests' Councils at its meeting every year enacts a litany of resolutions informing the American government how it ought to behave, without the slightest blush of modesty for its understanding very little of the complex problems involved in the issues on which it's giving the government its marching orders.

Why do priests think they can get away with such arrogance? I suspect the reason is that there is no built-in feedback mechanism structured into the ministry, no technique by which the laity can tell the clergy they don't know what they are talking about. Hence, a priest can say almost anything he wants on Sunday morning about politics, economics, family life, culture, teenagers or education and not be challenged by anyone. He assumes eventually that the lack of challenge means that people agree. Indeed, the pontificating priest doesn't even have a wife to tell him that he is full of beans.

Until priests are willing to impose upon themselves standards of professional performance, build feedback mechanisms into their ministry and take seriously the possibility that they are making fools out of themselves when they discuss topics about which they are uninformed, this lamentable arrogance will continue to be one of the biding problems of the presbyterate.

Problems of the Priesthood—III

Old Attitudes Prevail When a Priest is Appointed Pastor

The American presbyterate, more than a decade and a half after the Second Vatican Council, is still deeply troubled by the canonical mentality. Even those clergy who profess to be liberals or progressives and who take a sophisticated psychological approach to their ministry still are, without realizing it, victims of old canonical attitudes. An assignment is a benefice; when you receive the piece of paper from the chancery office that is your appointment, you own that assignment.

Most priests today might deny that they react this way, though their behavior makes a mockery of their denial. Some priests with sophisticated and advanced psychological training become the worst tyrants of all once they are appointed pastors. Everything they've learned in class and in the counseling room seems to slip away, and they fall into the patterns that they learned in their young priesthood. The parish is theirs. All relationships between priest and people which existed before they came are no longer valid. All customs, projects and programs which have been in the parish for years have no right to continue unless the new pastor approves them. Everything that has previously existed is to be swept away and the new man, now that he has a parish of his own, can do anything he wants.

I know of one parish, for example, that was, until the elderly pastor retired, one of the best parishes in the country. The day he arrived in the rectory, the new pastor, a man with sophisticated training, began to reshape the parish in his own image and likeness. In a short space of time, he'd edged the old pastor out of all activity, banished a former curate who'd helped on weekends, offended a considerable number of the active laity of the parish and chased teenagers out of the rectory.

The last move was the worst mistake of all. A teenager who answered the phone and opened the door at the rectory in the evenings had, by custom, brought many of his friends into the rectory office and the old pastor used to come down and discuss religion with them. The new pastor, oblivious to the needs of young people in the parish and apparently unaware that in most of the parishes of the Catholic Church priests would kill to have teenagers so available, instantly ordered the kids out of the rectory. It was his job, he said, to restore "order" to the parish, and he restored order without consulting for a moment with any of the laity of his parish. He had the right to do so, of course, because the parish was *his*.

Unfortunately, as lay people will tell you all over the country, this canonical mentality seems uneradicable in many priests. Indeed, it is almost a matter of principle to them that when they get a parish of their own, they must quickly undo all the work that previous priests have done and begin everything anew as though the parish had no past, no history, no tradition. Indeed, the typical priest is shocked when he is criticized for such behavior. The parish is his, isn't it? He can do whatever he wants with it, can't he?

It is an attitude that the medieval lords of the manor would have understood very well indeed.

Problems of the Priesthood—IV

Amateurism Keeps Priests from Improving

For several weeks I have been discussing bluntly and candidly (indeed, much too candidly for some priests and editors) the problems that are facing the Catholic priesthood in the United States. I see no point in pulling punches about these problems. The laity know all too well that the problems exist. The only ones who will be protected from a refusal to be honest are those clerics who deceive themselves about what the laity think. Charity, integrity and fidelity would all be violated by remaining silent on these problems.

In the last few weeks I have described the difficulties experienced by the priesthood because of disloyalty, arrogance and the canonical mentality. This week I shall discuss a fourth problem, amateurism, and then next week turn to the central cause of these other problems and suggest some tentative solutions.

A friend and colleague of mine, Professor Kevin Ryan of Ohio State University, is perhaps the country's most distinguished expert on the use of videotape feedback in teacher training. It is a simple enough matter to point a camera at a teacher and record the teacher's behavior before the classroom. Simple and devastating. The brilliance of Ryan's system is that it supports the teacher through the task of perceiving how poorly he/she is doing and then in a nonthreatening, encouraging and facilitating way, helps the teacher to improve.

I have repeatedly suggested to national and local groups of priests that Ryan's techniques and skills might be of considerable help in aiding the clergy to improve the quality of their preaching. Eighty percent of the Catholic laity in the United

States give priests poor marks on preaching. Most priests themselves are vaguely aware that they frequently don't do very well in the pulpit and yet no one, as far as I know, has ever approached Ryan seeking his help for priests' councils or priests' senates or priests' associations.

The conclusion is obvious. Priests are content (nervously content perhaps, but still content) with poor professional performance. They might vaguely like to be better preachers but they are afraid that they can't learn and content themselves with the reassuring nonsense that, well, there're other things that priests do that are important, too. The heads of the priests' senates of the country meet in national assemblies and pontificate on El Salvador and gun control. It does not occur to them, apparently, that strict justice is being violated in 80 percent of the pulpits of the Catholic Church in the United States every Sunday of the year.

The name of such professional sloppiness is amateurism. Many priests feel no motivation whatsoever to do well what they were ordained to do. Few, if any, parishes have feedback committees. Few, if any, dioceses have homiletic improvement programs and no one, as far as I know, has even bothered to read Ryan's articles on videotape training of teachers. If that isn't evidence that priests don't give much of a hoot about their professional performance, then I don't know what evidence can be found.

I am well aware of the enormous time demands that are made on priests. Yet, if one has to choose between staff meetings and homily preparation, there is no question as to how the priest should be spending his time. Indeed, there are very few things he does in his weekly work that are as important as homily preparation. Still, the homilies continue to be bad, the laity continues to complain and the amateurism of the priest continues to be a scandal.

Why such amateurism? The three problems I've discussed previously—disloyalty, arrogance and the canonical mentality—contribute to it. The envy of clerical culture reinforces mediocrity. Arrogance about the importance of the priesthood dispenses a man from the need to worry about how well he performs. If you have that piece of paper from the chancery office, it really doesn't matter how bad your Sunday homily is.

More deeply, however, there is no reward for excellent performance in the priesthood and there has been no training in the seminary to reinforce the sort of self-actualization that makes a man want to be good at what he does, regardless of whether he was rewarded for it. Thus, we come to what I take to be the core of the problem: The lack of self-esteem in the priest. To that I shall return next week.

A Payoff for
Professional Priests

As one who repeatedly has been critical of the professional performance of the Catholic clergy, I now propose to pay a compliment to priests who seem to be better than any other clergymen in playing the role of "confidant" to married women. One out of every seven young Catholic women does have some kind of confidant relationship with a priest that tends to make a considerable difference in her life, her personal happiness, her marital satisfaction and the marital satisfaction of her husband.

There is an especially interesting phenomenon that is involved in this hitherto uninvestigated aspect of Catholic life:

> While a confidant relationship with a priest does not seem to affect the sexual fulfillment of a woman in marriage, it does affect the sexual fulfillment of her husband (as reported in an independent questionnaire). Indeed, correlational analysis shows that this is the "intervening" variable between the confidant relationship and the marital satisfaction for the wife. Her relationship with the priest promotes sexual fulfillment of her husband and that in turn adds both to his and to her general marital satisfaction.

One must be extremely tentative in explanations of this fascinating phenomenon. It may be that "safe" relationship of reassurance and trust with another man that enhances the wife's self-esteem and confidence. It may be that the priest reassures her of the legitimacy of sexual pleasure in marriage. It may be that the priest simply provides the motivations that are so important in the critical *Kramer vs. Kramer* crisis years of the middle of the first decade of marriage.

The majority of those who have confidant relationships with priests are in favor of the ordination of women. The majority of those who do not have confidant relationships are not in favor of the ordination of women. This presumably establishes the "confidant" woman as adequately "liberal" on matters of clerical reform.

But the majority of the women in confidant relationships also support the continuation of clerical celibacy, while the majority of those who don't have confidant relationships support the possibility of a married clergy. The same thing is true of their husbands.

Might it be that the women in confidant relationships and their husbands both perceive—perhaps preconsciously—that it is precisely the celibacy of the priest that makes possible a beneficial confidant relationship? Might they not also support celibate women priests because of a preconscious insight that confidant relationships with such a person might also benefit husbands and indirectly wives?

Anyone who has been in the priest business for long and likes women (and a lot of priests, like a lot of other men, don't really like women, even though they may be sexually attracted to them) knows that there is a very subtle and powerful chemistry between the celibate priest and the married woman. It may be because each has powerful commitments to other realities that a certain electricity is possible between them that has a positive impact, surely, on the woman and, probably (if personal testimony means anything, I would say certainly), on the priest, too.

The chemistry in this relationship and the electricity it generates have been things that everybody has been afraid to talk about, partly out of fear that there was something wrong with them. Our research suggests tentatively just the opposite. There is a certain benign magic in a woman's relation to a celibate priest that makes a lot of marriages happier than they otherwise might be.

My praise of priests for this aspect of their professional performance may not be well received. It will offend the left wing, which wants celibacy abolished, and the right wing, which, convinced that priests ought to be hormoneless, resents any suggestion of a chemistry and an electricity between priests and women. However important, however delicate, however critical to the understanding of celibacy this finding might be, nobody is going to explore it any further.

What kind of priests do women seek out for confidants? They search for priests who are devout, democratic, concerned about the laity, well trained in the seminary and excellent preachers. They seek, in other words, not the touchy-feely, anti-intellectual slobs, but the professional.

Of Course Priests Fall in Love

At the risk of scandalizing both Catholics and anti-Catholics, I'm going to reveal a secret: Priests have hormones. They also have fantasies. They even fall in love. All of these phenomena cover an even more ugly secret: Priests are male members of the human race—and soon may include female members of the human race who also, be it noted, have hormones, fantasies and a propensity to fall in love.

In a TV interview about one of my novels, the woman newscaster opined that "for a priest" there was a lot of sex in the novel. There was not all that much sex, to tell the truth, and none of it was graphic or clinical or prurient (which may make it more erotic rather than less). She then added, "Of course priests don't fall in love."

To her dismay I replied that they sure do and that, to antic-
ipate her next question, I had fallen in love lots of times.

Human beings fall in love—in the sense of being powerfully
attracted to someone else. They also love—in the sense of form-
ing deep and lasting affection for someone else. At last count
priests were human beings. Why should they be thought to be
immune from these delightful, poignant, frustrating, discourag-
ing, disconcerting and fascinating experiences?

Why? Because the church for a long time has tried to pretend that priests were not human but some kind of super person.
The result is that we appear to many both in and outside the
church not to be more than human but less, ciphers, neuters,
hormoneless freaks.

Celibacy does not mean that one does not fall in love or
love; it rather means that one has made other commitments of
such importance that one does not end up in bed with those one
loves. Married men and women also fall in love; frequently it is
their spouse with whom they fall in love all over again in one of
the most delicious of all possible human romances, that of redis-
covering the beloved stranger. But other times their loves, often
sudden and transient, occasionally profound and durable, are
not their spouses. Yet infidelity usually does not occur and indeed is unthinkable because the basic commitments of their lives
are richer, more important and more rewarding. To pretend that
such reactions do not occur is absurd. To pretend that they are
not possible is cynical and ugly.

One of the principal reasons for having celibates in a community is to have a living proof that intense human emotional
attractions need not end up in the bedroom and indeed need not
even present a serious threat of doing so. The research finding
that celibate confidants can play a special role in strengthening
the marital satisfaction between a man and woman is, I believe,
based not on the fact that the priest has special things to say to
the wife, but on the fact that he is a special kind of person for
her—his existence opens up new possibilities in her marriage.
Far from being a non-erotic person, the good priest is a powerful erotic person in a community. Priests and laity would be a
lot better off and a lot happier if they could admit it. Those who

are not Catholic would understand a lot more about the nature of human nature if they could permit themselves to see it.

So, yeah, I have been in love often, sometimes for many years. Yet I have other commitments which are not really disturbed by such love and in fact are probably strengthened. Are the persons who so attract me unappealing as bed partners? Heavens no, they grow more appealing through the years and the decades (an interesting discovery, by the way). Has the fact that they are not bed partners and won't be caused some frustration? Well, yes, but then the opposite outcome would have produced its own variety of frustrations, as married people will surely testify. All love has its frustrations and its rewards.

The point is, however, that there are a wide variety of possible loves available to humans, all of them with their own rewards, challenges, excitements, frustrations and disappointments. We cannot have them all, we must pick and choose.

The reason for having around a celibate who is both faithful and loving is that he/she stands as evidence of the variety, the possibility and the choice.

CHURCH

I am often warned of the dangers of criticizing the church. I will shock the "simple laity" by "hanging out the dirty linen" and give comfort to anti-Catholics.

I should take a positive attitude toward the church, praise the good things and be silent about the bad.

That way I would prove that I love the church.

In fact there aren't any simple laity anymore, not after Humanae Vitae, *anyway*.

And the anti-Catholics know all about the Vatican Bank, Cardinal Cody's pension schemes and the machinations of the Pauline Fathers at Doylestown.

Those who want me to be silent about the weaknesses of church leaders should take up matters, as I suggested in the last section, with the authors of the New Testament, who were quite devastating in their descriptions of early church leaders.

Why are modern popes, cardinals and bishops immune from criticism when Peter and James and John were not?

And why must we pretend that the church is without blemish when the author of First Peter said that it was sometimes a fair bride and sometimes a whore?

Those who object to criticism on the grounds that it shocks the laity to know that priests and bishops are human and that the church has flaws assume that the laity are incapable of reading both the daily papers and fifteen minutes of church history.

Moreover, they are guilty of idolatry because they make the institutional church, not God, the object of their faith.

And they don't love the church.

For if you love the bride you want to make her more attractive for the returning bridegroom.

Ignoring Catholic History

How can you have a church in which tradition is important if history is unimportant? After all, is not tradition the history of the faithfuls' past beliefs and practices? How can we know what tradition is unless we know what Catholics have done at other times and other places? Their attitudes and behaviors may not be normative for us in different circumstances, but if the Lord's promise to protect the church from the gates of Hell is valid, then church practices in other times and in other places must be thought to embody the same tradition embodied in our beliefs and practices today.

I am not suggesting that history is the only source of tradition. Obviously one needs an interpreter if one is to understand the tradition. Yet, I wonder how you can have a tradition without history.

The approach of many Catholic leaders, and at least some Catholic laity, seems to assume that you could know what the tradition is (and has always been) without taking the slightest look at the historical record. One suspects this is so because history is messy, complex and confused, and such folks want their tradition neat, simple and clear.

For example, most Catholics have been told (and doubtless believe) that the Catholic Church never permitted remarriage after divorce. As Joseph Martos demonstrates in his new book on the history of the sacraments, *Doors to the Sacred*, in the seventh and eighth centuries a considerable number of Catholics, including popes and saints, were willing to approve remarriage after divorce for a number of reasons.

Saint Boniface in Germany, Saint Gregory in writing to Saint Boniface and Saint Augustine in England, for example, and church councils in France, England and Ireland all approved of remarriage after divorce in such circumstances as adultery, desertion, leprosy, abduction, freedom from slavery (a man could abandon a slave spouse if he was freed and marry a free woman, and vice versa) and disappearance in foreign wars. These are facts about which there is no historical dispute, not among historians, at any rate. They are on the public record, though that record is generally found to be somewhere deep in libraries.

I am not suggesting that it is now appropriate for the church to change its present disciplines and permit remarriage after divorce for reasons similar to those for permitting it in the early Middle Ages. There has been change, growth and development in the tradition, and there is no more point in going back uncritically to the past than there is in clinging uncritically to the present. To better evaluate the past or present, we should avoid fictional, not to say false, assertions about what the church has always done or has never done.

To slightly paraphrase Harry S. Truman, "Never say never because never is a terribly long time."

I would not charge ecclesiastical leaders with covering up, for example, the facts about Catholic marital disciplines. No one can cover up what he does not know. For most church leaders, including many of the clergy, Catholic traditions are what they were taught by their seminary textbooks whenever they happened to be in the seminary. If the writers of the seminary textbooks did not mention the letters of Pope Saint Gregory to Saint Boniface, the reason was they probably didn't know about such letters, either.

It may well be that seminarians are getting a better historical perspective than they did in the past, but I doubt it. It is much more logical that they are learning a slightly different but an oversimplified and prejudged version of the Catholic tradition. In the years ahead, when they become church leaders, they will resolutely repeat their seminary clichés just as the generation before them did.

It all works out, as long as you have a semiliterate laity who doesn't read history books and can't find the section in the library where one might learn about the marriage and divorce practices of the early Middle Ages. Unfortunately for those who are still relying on the oversimplifications of their seminary textbooks, we now have many lay people who know much more about the history of the Catholic position than do the clergy, to say nothing of the hierarchy. What happens to the credibility of the church when lay people who are aware of Pope Saint Gregory's letters to Saint Boniface on the subject of remarriage after divorce hear their pastor or the Vatican insist that the Catholic Church has never permitted remarriage after divorce?

What happens when the laity becomes painfully aware that church leadership is utterly ignorant of the complexities of Catholic tradition?

Vatican Money Crunch: The Inside Story—I

One of the things the Roman Curia might do to escape from its current money crunch is to build condominiums in the Vatican Gardens. It might also try to sell St. Peter's Basilica to Conoco. Short of such wild moves or brilliant imagination (of which the Curia is quite incapable), the crunch is likely to get much worse before it gets better.

The Roman Catholic Church is slowly going bankrupt. It is living off its capital. This year its financial deficit in lire is twice what it was two years ago—up from $20 million to $26 million in American dollars on a budget that is probably not in excess of $120 million.

The story behind the Vatican money crunch tells a lot about the organizational structure, the historical background and the crisis of confidence in contemporary Catholicism. Oddly enough, despite the horror stories you might have read or heard, neither incompetence nor corruption is responsible for the church's financial crisis.

For many centuries the church lived—as did every other institution in Europe—off the lands it owned. In retrospect, one might not approve of the church being among the largest landowners in Europe. One must face the fact, however, that for a millennium no one thought that such ownership was inappropriate.

When the Italian anti-clerical government wiped out the papal states, it confiscated all the papacy's land and left the Vatican literally impoverished—so much so that when Pope Benedict XV died in 1922, $100,000 had to be borrowed from an Italian bank to pay for his funeral expenses and the cost of the conclave that elected Pius XI.

Under the Lateran Treaty, which established the state of Vatican City, the Italian government paid the papacy $80 million in compensation for the land that had been seized, little more than a token restitution.

What about the fabled wealth of the Vatican? It is indeed fabled, that is to say fictional. St. Peter's may have a book value of $50 billion in that at least that much money would be needed to replace it, but it does not bring in income. Indeed, it is a white elephant, because it costs more to keep it in repair than the candle money income each year. Similarly, the upkeep of the Vatican Museum cancels out the admissions income each year. And there are no markets for secondhand basilicas or museums.

The money won in the Lateran Treaty became the Vatican's endowment and, together with the worldwide Peter's Pence collection, is the main source of Vatican income. It has been invested very well indeed since 1930, so that its value now is estimated as somewhere between $1.5 billion and $2 billion—less, be it noted, than the endowment of the Ford Foundation and not much more than that of Harvard University. Nonetheless, the growth of the endowment through investment indicates, as one broker put it to me, "they've done a lot better in the last fifty years than Morgan Stanley." And a lot better, one might add, than the Ford Foundation and the Harvard portfolio managers.

There have been some mistakes and some scandals, though probably less than in a comparable institution. The much talked-about "Sidona affair" did not notably injure the Vatican portfolio. (And incidentally, despite what you may have read, Bishop Paul Marcinkus of Cicero, Illinois, the president of the Institute for Religious Works, was not responsible for that affair, but took the heat for others. The Institute has its own investments, but is not responsible for the administration of the endowment.)

The Holy See has the operating capital of a medium-sized American foundation and has managed its financial affairs with both integrity and ability—in the narrow sense that it has not wasted its endowment funds. The crisis is the same as that facing any such institution. Inflation has sent costs—particularly labor costs—sky high, and investment income has not kept up with the costs.

This crisis has led the Curia to do two unthinkables—it has gone public with a financial statement and it is asking the rest of the world for help. Such a change may have a far greater long-term impact on the church than the Second Vatican Council.

The Vatican Money Crunch:
The Inside Story—II

The dire financial problems of the Catholic Church are caused not by the incompetence of those who manage the Vatican's modest endowment but by inflation. Indeed, the portfolio managers in Rome administer their funds (somewhere between $1.5 billion and $2 billion) with considerable skill; in a Curia notorious for its incompetence, the Vatican's investment supervisors seem to be competent professionals.

The church is running at a $26-million deficit this year for one very simple reason: Runaway inflation in Italy is wrecking the Vatican payroll budget. Curia officials don't make very much —the highest wage is that of a cardinal, which is under $10,000 a year. A Swiss Guard receives approximately $125 a month, a salary for which the fancy uniform is hardly much of a consolation.

There is no large-scale corruption in the Curia and has not been for a long time. But the tiny salaries make for petty corruptions, charges for dispensations, gifts, tips and small payoffs in return for appointments and favors that create a slightly tawdry atmosphere inside the Vatican. One wheeler-dealer American cardinal, for example, built his career, in substantial part, by passing out thousand-dollar Mass stipends to bureaucratic officials.

By attempting to live within its modest means, the Vatican then has produced an environment of poverty, sometimes pretty grungy poverty, which has had a demoralizing impact on the day-to-day operation of the Curia.

However, even penuriousness cannot hold back the hurricane of inflation for very long. Pope John Paul has not resisted the demands of Vatican employees for some kind of collective bargaining. Quite the contrary. Before he was wounded, he met with them and promised to respond to their demands and problems.

The establishment of an international commission of church leaders to design a solution to the Vatican money crunch is also part of John Paul's tough and courageous attempt to put the church back on a solid financial base. Yet the question remains: Why has an institution with almost eight hundred million members become so impoverished? Why haven't the wizards who administer the Vatican endowment thought up other sources of revenue?

There are two answers to that critical question. First of all, investing and fund-raising are quite distinct arts. Second, and much more important, the Curia has known all along that he who pays the piper will want to have a lot more to say about calling the tune. It prefers demoralizing poverty to the inevitable power-sharing that occurs when you go public with your financial statement and issue a desperate plea for help.

Of course, the foreign cardinals are not going to lay down a set of rules for the Curia as a condition for bailing it out. One cannot imagine men like Terence Cooke or John Krol behaving that way. But over the long haul the "foreigners" (meaning the non-curialists) will increase their power enormously in Rome as they pick up an ever-higher proportion of the tab. There will come new "foreigners" less malleable than current committee members who will want the decisions of the Vatican Council about "collegiality" (power-sharing between pope and bishops) taken seriously as a price for financial support. That will mean the beginning of the end of the half-millennium domination of the Catholic Church by the narrow, rigid and authoritarian Roman Curia.

And not a moment too soon.

Church Leaders as Media Symbols

Church leaders may not like to hear it, but their role as symbols is much more important than their role as administrators. The mass media almost automatically explain institutions in terms of the people that head them—a psychological and journalistic trick that Henry Luce introduced to modern America with his "Man of the Week" and "Man of the Year" cover stories.

You cannot, even in a half-hour or hour special, consider all the nuances and refinements of the problems facing a religious institution. But you can, even in a minute and a half, share with viewers and readers a feeling, an impression, a sense of what is happening, if you can observe or talk to a leader of the institution.

The name of the game is "incarnation" (with a small *i*, heretic hunters please note). Men represent the church, an idea that would not have been thought strange before the invention of the printing press and ought not to seem strange after the invention of TV.

Bishops are more important for the mass media and for those who are not of their denomination than they are for members of the denomination. The membership sees the parish clergyman on Sunday, and hence the bishop is not all that important a symbol for them. But the nonmembers and the media professionals don't have a parish clergyman of that denomination, and so the bishop is "theirs" in a sense that he is not to his own flock.

Churches are no different from any other institution with a powerful leader. The man on top becomes a "sacrament"—courtesy of the media—a "revelation" of what the institution stands for.

This symbolic function of the leader was overwhelmingly demonstrated in July 1982 when a new archbishop was appointed in Chicago. Overnight he became an instant celebrity, with hordes of reporters and cameramen following him down Michigan Avenue, into Holy Name Cathedral, inside his house and out to the seminary to witness a golf tournament. Interviews, profiles, in-depth stories and biographies filled the TV channels and the newspapers.

Indeed, the competition among journalists to report on, analyze, evaluate and interpret the new archbishop was fierce, so much so that one journalist was accused by his fellow journalists of breaking all the rules in a desperate attempt to salvage his fading career.

For the first time, the appointment of a new archbishop became a major media event, astonishing those around the archbishop and perhaps the new man himself.

And the photo of him in shirtsleeves at the golf tournament with a can of diet cola in his hand seems to have done more to win over the media and indeed his own congregation than anything else he might have said or done.

None of this has anything to do with the substance of his decisions or policies. Yet I would like to suggest that the picture of him with the cola can may be more important than any policy decision he might make in representing the church to the people of Chicago, especially those who are not Catholic.

I don't know whether religious leaders will be pleased at my suggestion that their gestures are more important than their substance. Yet almost anyone can be an administrator and a decision-maker and only very few people have the instinct for the right gesture—no amount of phony public relations gimmickry can create that instinct if it is not there (though intelligent advice can certainly enhance the effectiveness of the instinct).

Some churchmen refuse to deal with the press. Others try to fend it off or contain it or keep it at bay. Very few sense what a "bully pulpit" it can be, to use Theodore Roosevelt's term. One

has the impression that they figure they have none of the charisma of the late Archbishop Fulton Sheen and hence should stay
away from the TV camera as often as they can.

They don't understand that if you are a religious leader, you
have a lot of built-in charisma and you merely have to be, as a
beginning, honest and open and friendly.

And not afraid to be seen as a human being, Indeed so
human that you drink cola out of a can on a golf course.

On Advising Archbishops

The new archbishop of Chicago is being given all kinds of free
advice these days.

With characteristic narcissism a leader of the presbyterate
tells him that his most important problem is the morale of
priests.

And a leader of a liberal lay organization tells him that his
most important problems are finance and the rights of women.

And a letter writer in the *National Catholic Reporter* tells
him that the most important problems are where he lives, what
kind of transportation he rides in and what sort of food he eats.

And *The Wanderer,* with its sublime genius for the irrelevant, says that his most important problems are communion
under both species and shutting me up (the latter of which only
God can do).

I don't propose to offer him any advice—other than my
standard advice to all bishops that they break the rules of their
club and always tell the truth (advice that in the present structure of the church they cannot follow).

Nor do I propose to fight him unless I have to. One ordinary in a lifetime is enough to fight. If he leaves me alone, I'll
leave him alone.

But I do want to assert in the face of those who are so easy
with their free advice that the most serious problem facing the

American church is not clergy morale, or finance, or women, or episcopal palaces or limos or loudmouthed sociologists.

The most serious problem is rotten preaching.

And the second most serious problem is the decline of priestly vocations. And those problems are as critical in dioceses where there has been no conflict with the bishop as they are in Chicago.

Even in those dioceses where the bishop is a paragon of collegiality, even in those dioceses where the morale of the clergy is light years beyond that to be found on the shores of Lake Michigan, the laity still don't like the homilies they hear on Sunday, and the clergy and laity are still not seriously recruiting future priests.

In fact, in both matters, Chicago seems to be marginally better off than the rest of the country.

In part both problems may be related to clerical morale (though I think it more a problem of clerical self-esteem), but it is not the kind of problem that will be cured by the substitution of collective decision-making for autocracy.

The research evidence is clear on both issues: Even though the quality of Sunday preaching is the most important correlate of identification with the church, more than four fifths of the laity give us poor marks on our preaching.

And the most important reason for the decline of vocations is not celibacy but the absence of familial and clerical support for vocations.

Admittedly a lot more research is in order on what makes a homily effective and why priests and mothers are no longer encouraging vocations—and not the bargain-basement nonrandom sample research so dearly beloved by Catholic agencies.

But there is no point in doing this research unless and until the clergy and the hierarchy are willing to take their heads out of the sand and honestly face the reality of these two monumental problems, instead of banning this column whenever I say that the preaching of the American Catholic presbyterate is a disgrace, a violation of commutative justice and an abomination of desolation standing in the holy place.

And you can complain until Judgment Day about either the

celibacy rule (if you are a liberal) or the materialism of the young (if you are a conservative), and you do not thereby change the reality that the principal reason for the decline of vocations seems to be the decline of clerical enthusiasm for urging young men to follow them into the priesthood.

For about five years now I have been pleading in this column, in books, in articles and on the lecture platform for more attention to a) preaching and b) vocations.

And I get in far more trouble because of those pleas than I do because of my criticism of cardinals and my intolerably successful novels.

I think the response of both clergy and bishops to the problems of vocations and preaching is intellectually dishonest and morally corrupt. The bishops have indeed issued letters on preaching (and not unintelligent letters at that) and there have been occasional noises from priest groups on the same subject (when they are not trying to make foreign policy).

But if even half of what I claim the research shows is in fact true, the only valid responses would be crash programs on both recruiting and preaching (and programs involving high-quality research).

And of course such programs are not going to happen in Chicago.

Or anywhere else.

A "Terrible" Book That Won't Hurt the Church

I had a letter the other day from an archbishop friend of mine who had heard that I had written a "terrible novel" and expressed great fear that the "church would suffer" because of it. I don't know how terrible the novel is. One prepublication review termed it as "not lurid" and another said it was "tasteful." But I found the archbishop's model of what causes the church to suffer fascinating. Basically, the model presents the theory that the church suffers because of what priests and nuns and some lay people do. It never suffers, of course, because of what archbishops do, much less because of what the pope does. By definition in this model, church leadership cannot do anything that would cause the church to suffer; only followers can harm the church.

Implicit in the model is a picture of the typical Catholic lay person that I must say I find profoundly offensive, even though it is a picture that is often present in the minds of bishops and an older generation of clergy. The average lay person, it is presumed, is innocent, uneducated and easily scandalized. This sort of person ("one of the cap-and-sweater people," as one of my pastors described them) is incredibly naive about church leadership and church structure. He or she firmly believes that priests and bishops are devoid of human failings and that everything the church leadership does is wise, prudent, intelligent and motivated by the most lofty of concerns. Anyone who suggests that those in positions of influence and power in the church are less than archangels is thought to be scandalizing the "simple laity" and hence causing the church to suffer.

I do not doubt the existence of some such simple laity. I get a fair amount of mail from them and most of them are pretty nasty people who disapprove of everything that has happened since the Second Vatican Council. However, nothing that I say or do can scandalize them any more than they were scandalized by John XXIII or Paul VI, and any suffering that is imposed on the church because of their discontent has already long since been imposed.

The picture of the simple, naive, innocent, easily scandalized laity tells us more about the psychology of church leadership than it tells us about the actual condition of the laity. It is a convenient rhetorical device, an escape mechanism, for leaders who are afraid to face reality. It is all a marvelous inkblot into which they can project their own fears.

The church is going to suffer because of anything I say or do (especially when it is "tasteful" and "not lurid") when a fifth of the priests in the country have left the priesthood and married, religious orders have declined by 25 percent, when there is only one quarter of the seminarians that there were fifteen years ago, when more than 90 percent of the laity reject the church's birth control teaching, 80 percent the divorce teaching and 75 percent of the infallibility teaching?

Someone has to be kidding.

The mistakes, the incompetence, the brutalities, the insensitivities of church leaders in the last twenty years have caused so much suffering in the church that there is no room for any more. Leadership's failure to successfully implement the Second Vatican Council, the woeful inadequacy of the Vatican's press relations, John Paul II's failure to live up to his early promises, church leadership's corrosive inability to deal with problems of marital sexuality—none of these, apparently, caused the church to suffer at all, but a novel that admits that priests are human beings with problems and passions of their own, *that* will cause the church to suffer.

In fact, the typical lay person, no longer the simple, naive person who is going to be scandalized, is, according to empirical data, the person who has already been scandalized by the brutal insensitivity of church leadership and remains in the church despite that because, as one of my colleagues remarked, "It's my heritage and no one, no cardinal, no bishop, no pope, is going to take it away from me."

So with all due respect to the wonderful friend who was afraid that my "terrible novel" is going to cause the church to suffer, I would suggest that the scandal that has been caused by incompetent, harsh autocrats and unlistening church leaders in the last fifteen years has made it quite impossible for someone as trivially unimportant as me to hurt the church at all.

Some Dangerous Thoughts on Clothes

At the National Catholic Educational Association meeting this year there were nuns present who, for the first time, were not immediately identifiable as nuns. For until very recently, despite the abandonment of the religious habit, one could almost instantly spot a religious woman by the kind of clothes she wore.

Being utterly insensitive to the niceties of women's garb, I was unable to decide whether a woman at such a meeting was a nun or not. Some of my women students in my Sociology of Religion course, however, tell me that the shoes are a dead giveaway. Perhaps they are right.

Now come the dangerous thoughts:

1) Religious vocations in the orders of women declined about the same time that many, if not most, nuns gave up distinctive garb. Might there be a correlation? I am not suggesting necessarily that there is a correlation, but I think the question has to be raised. In the process of becoming "just like everyone else," did religious women lose the distinctiveness that was one of the important parts of their appeal? Heaven forbid that I should try to tell anyone, man or woman, what they ought to wear. But the sociological question of distinctiveness remains.

I fully concede that most of the religious "habits" were simply the ordinary garb of respect of women in the days when their communities were organized. Nonetheless, the sociological and symbolic importance of the religious habit was not considered seriously enough, it seems to me, when religious women abandoned such clothes. I do not suggest that they return to such outmoded dress. Nonetheless, I think it important that the question of distinctiveness be faced once again. If nuns are "just like everyone else," is there any reason to believe that they will attract new recruits?

2) One of the great unmentionable secrets in American Catholicism is the fun that Catholic laywomen frequently make of the "dowdiness" (a nasty word and I don't like to use it, but if I am to accurately report the reaction, that is the word I must use) of sisters wearing lay garb. Personally, I think it is monstrously unfair of laywomen to say these things behind the backs of sisters and never say them to their faces. However, such fun-poking (and

in my judgment, it's pandemic) is no help to the religious communities of women in their search for vocations.

3) One could go further and say that there is nothing
wrong with a bride of Christ looking chic. That, in fact,
is the way she ought to look. Should it be tolerated for
religious women to be any less presentable and attractive than business and professional women that one in-
creasingly sees in the airports of the country? Ought not
brides of Christ, in fact, be at least as attractive in their
dress as other women? Do not tell me that chic garb
costs too much money when a considerable number of
American women are able to dress attractively on very
tight budgets.

One suspects that admonitions against vanity in a novitiate
and ideological feminism persuaded many religious women that
personal attractiveness is not important. I am sorry, but God designed human beings to look attractive, and both men and
women ought to cooperate with the divine plan. It is virtuous
for all women (and all men, too) to look as sharp as they possibly can. A religious commitment, far from diminishing the importance of that person, seems to me to increase it.

I suppose the roof will fall in on me for writing this, but I
don't care. It's high time somebody said it and I warn one and
all that all nasty letters of protest will go straight in the waste-
basket.

The Church's
Evolving Tradition

One of the problems facing American Catholicism is the fundamental dishonesty of those who purport to speak for the Catholic tradition. Thus, we are resolutely told by our church leaders

and teachers that women have never been ordained, the church has always condemned birth control and that Catholicism has never recognized divorce.

In fact, it seems very likely that women have not only been priests but bishops. Theodora of Smyrna, it seems very likely, performed the roles of a bishop, and Saint Bridget of Kildare (my favorite saint in all the world) apparently ordained priests at her coed monastery. Bridget may not have been a bishop, but you would have been in trouble if you tried to tell her she wasn't—which has been the case for anyone who tried to put an Irish woman in her place through the whole course of human history.

Moreover, all through the nineteenth century, the church downplayed its teaching on birth control, often explicitly refusing to discuss the matter. In discreet and secret replies to the bishops of France, the Holy Office advised them to proceed very cautiously lest they disturb the conscience of married people, and Pope Leo XIII wrote his encyclical on Christian marriage precisely at the time when birth control was almost universal in France without ever once mentioning the subject.

Finally, for the first thousand years of Christian history, marriage was not regulated by the church, but by the civil authorities, and civil authority, even in Christian times, permitted divorce by mutual consent. As Dr. Joseph Martos notes in his monumental book *Doors to the Sacred* (a history of the sacraments of the Catholic Church), even church leaders were tolerant of divorce up to the early Middle Ages.

Across the Irish Sea, the Irish church permitted husbands of unfaithful wives to remarry and other Irish laws advised against remarriage but did not forbid it. In eighth-century France, men whose wives committed adultery were allowed to remarry. Wives whose husbands contracted leprosy were also permitted to remarry if their husbands gave consent. Pope Gregory II, in 726, advised Saint Boniface of Germany that if a wife was too sick to have intercourse with her husband, the husband might take another wife while he took care of the first one. Saint Boniface, for his part, recognized desertion, adultery and entrance into a monastery as grounds for divorce.

Now let it be clear: I am not advocating a return to any of

these practices, nor rejecting the present teaching of the church on any of these matters. I am simply asserting that it is false, ignorant and dishonest to contend that the present church disciplines have been honored always in Catholic history. The Catholic tradition is much more pluralistic, flexible and mutable than those who write the textbooks and the Vatican decrees are prepared to admit. To such leaders and teachers, the tradition usually means what they learned in their textbooks when they were in the seminary twenty-five or thirty years ago.

For example, the bishop of Brooklyn forbids an individual to act as a sponsor in a baptism. His decision may well be correct in terms of the present church discipline, but it's utterly absurd to claim that the same decision would have been made always and everywhere in Catholic history. There may be many excellent reasons for the present discipline. If there are, let these reasons be advanced and let the present rules be defended on their merits. But do not defend this act on the grounds that things were always the same. They weren't.

The Catholic Church once permitted divorce and remarriage. It was once remarkably tolerant (though never, it would seem, approving) of contraceptives. It once allowed married priests and it once apparently ordained women, not only as priests but even as bishops. Such truths may be unpalatable facts to both church leaders and to conservative Catholics, but those who attempt to cover them up in the name of protecting the Catholic laity from scandal are, in fact, lying.

Greeley's Third Law

I propound to you for your reflection, gentle souls, Greeley's (Third) Law: There is an inverse correlation between the vitality of a Catholic organization and the militancy of its social action rhetoric.

It can also be called the Law of Catholic Institutions: The more relevant the rhetoric, the more irrelevant the institution.

Or to put it more bluntly: A sure sign of the near liquidation of a Catholic institution is when those who are presiding over the institution expend most of their energies telling the leaders of other institutions how to solve their problems.

These remarks are occasioned by the unintentional hilarity of the Conference of Major Superiors of Men in Milwaukee, Wisconsin, recently. Few will dispute that the religious life is in a terrible crisis, one of the most serious since Benedict of Nursia. How did the superiors react?

Well, they passed a lot of resolutions. They condemned the neutron bomb, the Reagan budget, the involvement of the United States in El Salvador and the increase in military spending. They endorsed gun control and the Equal Rights Amendment.

See what I mean?

Now, I happen to agree with most of these stands. I don't like Reagan and I don't like the neutron bomb (or the machine gun or gunpowder, as far as that goes) and I'm for equal rights and gun control.

But you know what? I don't need religious superiors to tell me about these things and I don't think anyone else does, either. I doubt that their resolutions will affect a single vote in Congress or change the mind of a single citizen, indeed of a single member of their own communities. The only result of such resolutions is to make the men who vote for them feel virtuous.

And another name for it is "cheap grace"—virtue acquired without any effort.

If one is to judge by the sympathetic press accounts of the meeting, the problems of the religious life are to be solved by recasting the founders as contemporary social activists. Vocations will be found, morale restored, direction will be re-established, vision created by repeating the shallow clichés of the "peace and justice" faddists.

How much do you want to bet?

I'm for social justice, though I detected in the documents and speeches coming out of the Milwaukee debacle no awareness that there is a unique Catholic contribution to the "reconstruction of the social order"—to quote the name of the great encyclical (authored by a religious, incidentally) whose fiftieth anniversary went unnoticed by the major superiors.

What can you do with a group of men who prate about social justice and are unaware of the anniversary of *Quadragesimo Anno* and say not a word about the principle of subsidiarity?

Me, I'm not a religious, but I believe in the religious life, apparently more than the superiors do. I don't think its future (the subject of the meeting) will be shaped by the repetition of liberal clichés and the passing of resolutions. No institution that has served human needs for fifteen hundred years can be undone, even by the most stupid leadership.

But the picture of the successors of Benedict and Frances, Bonaventure and Thomas, Ignatius and Vincent, sounding like editorials from the Washington *Post* or *The Nation* of six months ago is dismaying. I shall be candid: They are blind and the leaders of the blind, a disgrace to the traditions they caricature. The religious life will survive them, through no fault of theirs.

It reminds me of the rejoinder to an intellectual who complained about the Boston Irish priest who preached on sins of sex but not on concentration camps: Few of the man's parishioners would commit a concentration camp. Similarly, one wonders how many of the members of the religious communities whose leaders came to Milwaukee are going to commit a neutron bomb. Or carry a Saturday Night Special.

Doubtless some of the superiors will renew their efforts to have this column banned. More power to them, say I. Everyone's rights are important, except the rights of those who dare to say that the major superiors not only don't have Roman collars but, like the emperor, have no clothes at all.

In Defense of Cardinal Cooke

I want to end this year by rising to the defense of a cardinal prince of the church, New York's Terence Cooke.

Recently the cardinal had some things to say about the morality of nuclear deterrence that could be interpreted as a disagreement with the fuzzy sentiments on the same subject uttered at the bishops' meeting in November.

Mind you, the cardinal was not advocating dropping a bomb on the parade ground of the Kremlin or anything of the sort. He merely said that under some circumstances, it wasn't necessary to engage in unilateral disarmament and thus turn the world over to the Russians so they can convert the planet into one huge Poland.

A group of New York radicals promptly jumped all over him, accusing him of breaking ranks with his fellow bishops on the issue of world peace.

Now, I'm not really sure that he did. If he had proposed his statement at the meeting of the lords spiritual, it would have been enthusiastically endorsed, just as was the staff-prepared statement on nuclear war. Bishops tend to vote for anything that anyone responsible proposes at their meetings, so long as it doesn't have to do with sex.

But let's concede for the sake of argument that the cardinal had the courage of his convictions and really was breaking ranks with other bishops. Would that be wrong? Is it proper for those who claim to be liberals or radicals to demand that one bishop agree with other bishops publicly, even if he thinks they are wrong? Is it not the case that the same radicals who blasted the cardinal for apparent disagreement with the majority would have been lavish in their praise of him, if, for example, he should break ranks on the subject of the ordination of women?

In other words, you must go along with your peers in the hierarchy when the radicals happen to agree with your peers, and you must break ranks when they happen to disagree.

And if a bishop is to be constrained to accept the teaching of the national hierarchy, ought not the laity and the clergy be constrained to accept the teaching of their bishop? If Cardinal Cooke cannot disagree with other bishops, by what right do his critics within his own diocese disagree with him?

Freedom for me but not for you.

The document attacking the cardinal is curious; it might just as well have been written in Moscow. It describes as a "fiction" the cardinal's contention that the American government has sincerely tried for nuclear disarmament.

It isn't a fiction, but only the most naive dupes of Russian propaganda or American self-hatred could possibly say that it is. You may well criticize the ineptness of the American disarmament effort—as Senator Daniel P. Moynihan, of New York, did in a brilliant *New Yorker* article last year. But don't deny that efforts have been made by every American president since Dwight Eisenhower (Mr. Reagan included, though perhaps just barely).

The problem with the unilateralists, including the bishop unilateralists (if there really are any beyond the language of staff documents), is that they are irresponsible in the strict sense of the word. Knowing that they will not be taken seriously, they are under no obligation to take into account the consequences of their proposals being adopted.

They can revel in their own moral purity and know that the Red Army will never drag them out of their homes late at night.

How can one tell whether a unilateralist is being responsible? I propose two tests:

1) Is he willing to admit the possibility that this moral position, if adopted by the United States, might lead rather quickly to a third world war? If he/she isn't willing to face that possibility, then she/he isn't being honest. I don't mean that the unilateralist must say that this is certain to happen as Russia grabs for world power. I merely mean that the unilateralist is willing to consider it a possibility that must go into the moral calculus.

2) Is the unilateralist willing to offer an explanation as to why deterrence has enforced the longest period of peace that Europe has ever known? I don't know quite what to make of this phenomenon; it is weird that terror should bring peace when love and rationality cannot. Moreover, it is a peace purchased at an enormous price in potential disaster. Yet it is still peace, however risky. I don't think any serious student of European geopolitics doubts that there would have been a long and destructive war be-

tween the Soviet Union and the United States in the last forty years if it had not been for the bomb. Never before have two such massive armies faced each other across a border and not gone to war.

The phenomenon has to be talked about in any discussion of world problems. Until they show some comprehension of the world's ambiguities and complexities, the sophomoric unilateralists, whether they be bishops or the critics of bishops, do not deserve a serious audience.

Good Catholic Art Highlights Religious Traditions

"Why don't you people make stained glass windows or paintings or frescoes anymore?" an Episcopalian woman asked me recently. "My kids and I just came back from Italy and I think I gave them a complete course in Christianity by explaining the meanings of the paintings and the frescoes and the stained glass. And that was without our going to France and seeing the cathedrals there."

I didn't explain to the woman that Catholics now are no longer into the making of images and that many of our new churches are almost as devoid of imagery as are strict fundamentalist Protestant churches. Just when the world rediscovered the importance of religious imagination, we Catholics decided it was unimportant and have turned our attention instead to revolution, Marxism and radical feminism.

Another manifestation of Greeley's (First) Law: When Catholics forget something, other people remember it.

One must be candid: Catholic church art in the United States is unspeakably bad, even worse than Catholic church music. The religious faith that produced Notre Dame de Paris and *The Last Judgment* and the Rose Window at Chartres now produces obscure drivel. Even the sentimental glossy prints of an earlier era have vanished, to be replaced either by nothing at all or by vigorously "nonrepresentational" junk, which makes the average lay person laugh until he thinks about how much it costs, and then makes him cry.

I have nothing against modern art. On the contrary, I always try to visit the Guggenheim Museum when I am in New York, and I will enthusiastically applaud any effort to use the same artistic methods and perspectives for religious purposes, as long as the works which result are good. The only trouble with most modern Catholic religious art is the results are terrible. Witness the horrendous monstrosity in the papal audience hall in Rome, a twisted chunk of metal that must make John Paul wince every time he walks down the aisle.

The fundamental difference, I fear, between many of those engaged in modern religious art and their predecessors is that the moderns are interested in expressing their personalities and the older masters were interested in telling a religious story, a story containing an implicit but powerful religious vision. One need only consider the stained glass windows of the Gothic cathedrals or the pages of the Book of Kells to realize that use of art as a means of religious instruction (or the telling of a story) can be very great art indeed and can reveal the artist's own unique vision with great power and effectiveness.

But somehow, since those days, the self-image of the artist has changed and also the church's convictions about how important art is for passing on a religious heritage. If you have schools and textbooks and religious instruction classes and teachers and directors of religious education and all the other paraphernalia of a modern parish (of whatever denomination), who needs paintings, frescoes and stained glass?

The common assumption, then, of the religious educational establishment is that the page of catechism or textbook beautifully explained by a teacher to a twelve-year-old or a sixteen-year-old is far more important religiously than a mother telling a four-year-old about Joseph and Patrick and Guadalupe and Hedwig and all the other characters who used to inhabit our churches.

In fact, just the opposite seems to be the case. The mother or the father explaining pictures and images in the church has a far more powerful religious influence than does the classroom instruction five or ten years later.

How Scary Is the Electronic Church?

The electronic church has a lot of people worried these days. The seeming success of the Sunday morning gospel programs, fundamentalist in doctrine and far right in politics, terrifies liberals, ecclesiastical or secular, especially because the electronic church is closely linked to the Moral Majority, and the Reverend Jerry Falwell seems to have his strong foot solidly planted in both of them.

The articles one reads on the electronic church are curious. Most commentators are willing to take at face value the audience claims of the Sunday morning evangelists and to view with alarm their great income, their extraordinary influence and their immense political potential. Such articles routinely warn of the ever-increasing possible audience for the electronic church as cable TV and satellite networks link more and more homes into the electronic congregation.

It's often hard to know what the purpose of these articles is other than to scare the readers and perhaps build an environment in which the electronic church might eventually be deprived of its tax-exempt status. But how scary is the electronic church? How much power does it have? How much political clout is it able to deliver? What difference does it really make either politically or religiously in American life?

Professor William Martin of Rice University, probably one of the most creative and imaginative sociologists in America, has been monitoring the various radio and TV fundamentalist preachers for a long time, and his conclusions are much less scary than those offered by most commentators on electronic Christianity.

Professor Martin notes that on any given Sunday the electronic congregation involves no more than twelve or thirteen million people; that these people are fundamentalists in their religious orientation and conservative in their political orientation to begin with. The electronic church seems to be preaching to the saved and not winning converts from the unsaved. Right-wing Christian TV programs are successful because right-wing Christians watch TV and not vice versa.

Moreover, according to Professor Martin, the Sunday morning evangelists are losing some of their popularity. It would appear that on the average there has been approximately a 10 percent decline in the size of the various congregations of the different preachers in the last year. Precisely at the time when, according to the scare stories, the electronic church and the Moral Majority are becoming a national political threat, the size of their Sunday morning congregation declines. This is not exactly the behavior of a group which constitutes a major political threat to American life.

The truth is that since the invention of radio there has been a substantial audience, perhaps 10 percent of the American public, for fundamentalist electronic preachers. There is no particular reason to believe, if one considers the data carefully, that these preachers are any more important or powerful than they ever were—which is not to say that they are unimportant, but merely that the national media never noticed them before. A scholar like Professor Martin, who for years has tried to call attention to the electronic church, now suddenly finds himself in the position of trying, in the name of truth and accuracy, to warn that they are not as important or as terrible as some liberal paranoids would like to believe.

I do not find the theology in the electronic church particularly attractive. There is perhaps some reason to be skeptical about the financial hustle in which some of the electronic clergymen engage. Yet, this is a free country and they are exercising their freedom of speech and their congregation is exercising its freedom to listen. If you ask me, I think the journalists and commentators who are not careful with the facts about the electronic church are much more of a menace than the TV evangelists.

The Catholic Church Needs Fiscal Competents

With all its other problems, the Catholic Church in the United States faces a looming crisis of fiscal credibility. The crisis is based on the fact that there is very little accountability in Catholic organizations and institutions for the use of funds.

Most Catholic dioceses, religious orders and other institutions are administered with integrity and responsibility, if without much imagination. Some others are absolute models of the careful and responsible probity that ought to mark any institution that assumes the public trust for the use of the money of its members. Unfortunately, there are some Catholic institutions in which the fiscal and financial policies are incompetent, irresponsible and even corrupt. Since corruption is news and probity isn't, the image of the many is often badly tarnished by the performance of the few.

Minor mistakes and relatively small thefts (which at times can run into six figures) are inevitable in any organization that deals with a large and regular flow of money—as bank executives will surely testify, at least in their more relaxed and unthreatened moments. Such lapses and losses are regrettable, but they do not constitute a long-range problem, either in public image or in financial accountability.

The problem of financial credibility for the Catholic Church, rather, is the result of enormous losses, running into the many millions of dollars, that have plagued certain religious orders and certain dioceses for the last several years. Sometimes the losses are the results of well-meaning incompetence. A new bishop arrives on the scene to find the attorney general of the state ready with a financial lien because the diocese is so heavily in debt. (One bishop told me that it took him over a year merely to stop the hemorrhage of funds from his diocese.) He is then faced with the unpopular and destructive responsibility of paying off the debt his predecessor built up without bothering to tell his clergy and people about it.

A second problem—and more serious in its motivations if not in its outcome—is the situation that arises particularly in a religious community when an enthusiastic but not well-balanced fundraiser becomes involved in problematic financial wheeling and dealing, often including personal high living and high rolling. Such well-publicized scandals, some of which seem to come dangerously close to violating mail fraud laws, go beyond mere incompetence and strongly suggest financial corruption.

Worst of all, especially when it's combined with the two preceding patterns, is the situation in which a bishop or religious superior, so closely identifying himself or herself with the institution over whose funds he or she has trust, comes to believe that he or she can do absolutely anything with the entrusted funds. "I am the diocese," or "I am the order," says such a leader, and plays with vast sums of money like they were the contents of his/her own personal petty cash box.

I am not suggesting that there are very many such situations in the church. Unfortunately, only a few scandals are enough to impugn the integrity and credibility of everyone else.

The fundamental reason for the problem is the lack of any financial accountability. A bishop or a religious superior is really never reviewed by any outside agency, inside the church or outside the church, unless he or she chooses voluntarily to submit to such a review. In the absence of full and public accountability, human weakness and human ignorance and human malice have too much freedom. Whatever is to be said about the case of the Pauline Fathers in Pennsylvania and their financial troubles, I will confess that I was shocked (and things that happen in the church rarely shock me anymore) by the ease with which some bishops promptly and cheerfully contributed $1 million of their dioceses' funds as gifts to bail out the troubled religious order.

The people who contributed that money on Sunday morning to their parishes were not consulted and very likely would not have agreed to have picked up the tab for bills incurred by high-living, high-rolling clergymen of whom they had never heard.

No one, not even Rome itself, really has any idea of how ecclesiastical funds are spent in the United States. Often the published diocesan reports are masterpieces in deliberate obscurity. If the overwhelming majority of honest, hard-working, careful, prudent and responsible leaders in the Catholic Church do not want to be smeared by the wheeler-dealers, the high rollers and the incompetents, they had better devise a system of financial accountability quickly.

Mary an Ecumenical Asset?

A couple of years ago I went with a crowd of friends to see John R. Powers' play *Patent Leather Shoes,* based on his novel about the Catholicism of the 1950s. In one scene the second graders of St. Christina's School in Chicago are doing the annual May crowning. They begin to sing the traditional May crowning hymn, "Bring Flowers of the Rarest."

At the chorus, the whole audience joined in "O Mary we crown thee with blossoms today, Queen of the Angels, Queen of the May." Some Jewish people sitting near me were humming (ethnic group loyalty in favor of a Jewish mother?). On the way out I cornered the gifted young playwright. "Do they do it every night, John?"

"Since the first night," he replied. "If they ever stop doing it we'll be worried."

The experience was one more confirmation of something I've suspected for a long time: Mary, the mother of Jesus, is one of the greatest assets Catholic Christianity has. Henry Adams was right when he said that, as the most important symbol in fifteen hundred years of Christianity, Mary held together Western culture. Many of the top thinkers and teachers in Catholicism have abandoned Mary in a concession to ecumenism, a concession some Protestant thinkers and teachers seem to demand.

The New York *Times* has repeatedly described Pope John Paul II as a "conservative" because of his devotion to Mary. Yet a recent study of 2,500 young Catholics indicates that the Mary image still is powerful in their imagination, more powerful than the God image or the Jesus image.

Nor is Mary irrelevant, as some Catholic elitists have thought. A strong Mary image correlates with sexual fulfillment in marriage, a commitment to social concern and racial justice and, for men, support for the ordination of women. There is no evidence that it correlates with sexual narrowness or repression.

In fact, our research shows that the Mary image emphasizes for young Catholics the fact that God loves us with the tenderness, the sensitivity and the compassion of a mother. It encodes a pleasant experience of mother love in childhood and links that experience with a pleasant experience of a loving spouse in adult life. This connection, mind you, is sociological fact and not doctrinal belief.

Mary represents the womanliness of God as revealed in the womanliness of maternal love.

For Catholics only, you say?

It would seem not. There were several hundred non-Catholics in our sample—Protestants, Jews and others who were married to Catholic spouses. While 65 percent of the Catholics had high scores on our "Madonna" scale, so too did 40 percent of our non-Catholic spouses—more than half of the Baptists and Methodists and 37 percent of those who had no religion at all.

There may be differences across denominational lines in doctrinal teachings about Mary. There seems to be much less difference in imaginative pictures. The pictures come before the doctrines and have a much greater impact on matters as diverse as prayer and the search for racial justice.

So those who jettisoned Mary for ecumenical purposes were mistaken. She is an asset for ecumenism and not a liability.

She is, after all, the only one left in the marketplace who can play the role of a mother goddess—a revelation of the ultimate maternal love. All the other competitors—Venus, Nut and Astarte—have long since gone.

I cannot escape the melancholy conclusion, however, that as in so many other matters, Catholic leaders and thinkers are too dumb to know what a resource they have in the image of a Jewish mother whom humans have honored for more than fifteen hundred years.

Harris Poll Shows Lingering Anti-Catholicism

Pollster Lou Harris is the only one in the trade who takes seriously the persistence of anti-Catholicism in the United States. He has done surveys on the subject and has spoken out personally about the implications of his findings. No one pays much attention to him, but still Mr. Harris is to be commended for his courage. It is not fashionable to speak about this third American prejudice (the others are racism and anti-Semitism), which may be the most intractable of the three.

It would appear from Mr. Harris' published reports that about one fourth of the nation has some kind of anti-Catholic sentiment. It is strongest not in the South but in the Northeast, and not among conservatives but among self-defined "liberals"— though it is not strong among Jews (despite the fact that they tend to be both "liberal" and live in the Northeast).

There is no evidence to measure whether anti-Catholic prejudice is increasing or decreasing. There are no questions comparable to the ones Mr. Harris uses for which we have answers from five or ten years ago. My impression is that it is on the rise, particularly since the journey of Pope John Paul to the United States.

I've been inundated with phone calls from media types planning to do "specials" on the state of the church, most of them grimly determined to prove that the papal visit was a "failure" and a "disaster" for American Catholics. I patiently tell them that the empirical evidence supports neither their interpretation of the pope as an archreactionary nor their theory of crisis in the American church.

I insist that American Catholics can admire the pope and turn him off on certain topics with relatively little strain. I say that identification with the church is twice as likely to be affected by the quality of sermons in your local parish than it is by such issues as abortion, birth control, divorce, celibacy and the ordination of women put together. They react as though I'm making up the findings.

One fellow from the Dick Cavett program was furious at me for not wanting to go on the program with a flake from the far right and a flake from the far left. He told me that I was guilty of censorship because together with other "prelates" (an unsought promotion) I wouldn't go on the air with the left-wing flake. He read me a long lecture about the number of young people who were not practicing the faith—serenely unaware that I'd done the research on the subject. When I told him that his approach might be good entertainment but would not lead to serious discussion, he hung up in anger.

And a man from the Canadian Broadcasting Corporation asked me as a lead-off question whether I knew of any Catholic psychiatrist who would go on TV to discuss the negative impact on marital happiness of Catholic sexual morality. I told him that there was no evidence in the literature to suggest such an impact, he railed at me about convent schools. I told him there were few such left and those that still existed were turning out feminists. He began shouting about the convent school his mother attended.

No statute of limitations, it would seem.

Then there is the person from an American network who called a friend of mine to get information for a one-hour special about the "divisiveness" of John Paul—the decision has apparently already been made that he's divisive.

This sort of mentality, widespread in the elite media, is the reason why one must go to European journals like the London *Tablet* or the Paris *Le Monde* for accurate Vatican news.

Or consider Charles Sailer's best-selling paperback, *Second Son*. It asks us to believe that God sends another messiah into the world to repeat the message of Jesus. With a considerable pretense at knowing how the Vatican works from the inside, the book then tells us that an international Vatican underground at first kidnaps the new son of God and then has him executed. Writer and publisher have so far got away with this bigotry unscathed.

Since they don't read much (some of them don't know how to read or write) the official Catholic leadership doesn't know about the book. And those "liberals" concerned with bigotry and prejudice are not disturbed. After all, it is at least likely, one hears them say, that the Vatican does have such international web of secret agents. Probably with a Mafia link-up. Mr. Sailer knows his audience well—an audience of men and women sufficiently bigoted to believe anything about Catholicism.

I expect any day now a paperback edition (probably from Beacon Press) of that classic of nineteenth-century nativism, *The Awful Revelations of Maria Monk.*

The New York Review of Books will probably be able to find some Jesuit to write a favorable review of it.

Witch-hunts Always Fail

Let's take a look at some of the people who have been condemned by the Catholic Church in the last century and a half.

Antonio Rosmini: A northern Italian genius who was on the verge of being made a cardinal, but he fell out of favor with Pius IX and his books were placed on the Index. He preached a Christianity of intense charity, strong cultural commitment and vigorous democratic political participation. He is now praised as one of the great thinkers of the nineteenth century and had an enormous influence on Albino Luciani—John Paul I.

John Henry Newman: His magazine was suppressed and his ideas put under suspicion of heresy. He lived for many years, as he himself put it, "under a cloud." He died a cardinal and was often described as the "invisible father" of the Second Vatican Council.

Maurice Blondel: A blind French lay philosopher who tried to reconcile religion with scientific progress. Never formally condemned, he was under constant suspicion and harassed by ecclesiastical witch-hunters. Today no one denies Blondel's enormous positive influence on Catholicism.

J. M. LaGrange: The first of the great French Catholic Scripture scholars. His books were withdrawn from circulation and he was forbidden to write any new ones. Now he is hailed as the father of the Catholic scriptural revival. His pupils (including the great Cardinal Bea) helped to shape the Second Vatican Council.

Pierre Teilhard de Chardin: A French scientist, mystic and philosopher. He was forbidden repeatedly to publish and was forced into exile. He died in a run-down hotel in New York because there was no room for him in a Jesuit house. He was rehabilitated by Pope John XXIII, and his books have sold in many languages. He is now hailed as a great Catholic thinker.

Henri DeLubac: Jesuit theologian. Forced to give up teaching and withdraw his most important book from circulation. He is now universally hailed as a great Catholic teacher.

Yves J. M. Congar: French Dominican theologian. Forbidden to teach or publish and sent into exile because of his books on ecumenism and reform in the church. His health was ruined in exile. He is often hailed as the architect of Vatican II because his two books (though forced out of circulation) were virtually taken over in conciliar documents, many of which he wrote. Reported to be Pope John Paul II's favorite theologian.

John Courtney Murray: American Jesuit. He was forbidden to write or teach on the subject of the relationship between church and state and "disinvited" from the first session of the Second Vatican Council. He came to the other sessions, wrote the document on religious liberty, and concelebrated Mass with the pope at the end of the council.

One could easily double or triple this list of names of distinguished and important Catholic scholars who have been harassed, silenced, exiled, banned, condemned and otherwise punished by the church. All have been rehabilitated, praised and even celebrated—usually after they're dead, though if they live long enough (like Newman) or are lucky (like Murray), while they're still alive.

A number of conclusions seem to follow:

1) Even though it is a risky and dangerous vocation to be a scholar and thinker in the church, there have been and still are men who are willing to make that commitment, no matter what happens. Catholicism and scholarship are not incompatible, but the church has in the past and still now gives its scholars a hell of a hard time. That there are enough men (and now women) who are willing to take their chances on posthumous rehabilitation is evidence of the passionate commitment Catholicism still generates.

2) All of these folk were tormented and harassed on the grounds that their work was a threat to the belief of the faithful or a challenge to the pure doctrine of the Catholic faith. In each case, the judgment of a later generation was that they were no such thing.

3) In almost every case they were the victims of clerical envy that distorted their teaching and writing. They were also the victims of witch-hunts generated by political power plays. The guise of "protecting" or "defending" the faith may have been, in some cases, sincere; but envy often thinks it's sincere.

4) Witch-hunts don't work. The hunters invariably lose and the hunted win—if only in the long run (the long run in which often they are dead). The witch-hunters may destroy the persons and even the lives of their victims. They may impede and limit the contributions the victims could have made. But the work of the victims survives and the work of the witch-hunters is finally consigned to contemptible oblivion.

5) The church needs a new system to relate to its scholars, one that is free of the workings of envy and the lust for power of petty bureaucrats. The present system does not

work, not even by the standards of the most reactionary witch-hunters. The victims may be destroyed, but they almost always win anyhow.

Even Galileo did.

Secrecy Means Financial Problems for the Church

The Catholic Church continues to have enormous problems because it cannot bring itself to conduct its financial affairs in the light of day, on the housetops, as Jesus said was the place for his followers to do their work. On the contrary, the church's obsessive passion for secrecy continues to cause it terrible problems, as two recent incidents have demonstrated.

Archbishop Paul Marcinkus, the president of both Vatican City and the Vatican Bank, has been receiving a bum rap in the American press about a mysterious financial scandal that allegedly involves the Institute for Religious Work, as the Vatican Bank is called.

Actually, curial enemies of the Cicero, Illinois, native have been trying to do him in for years. They leak stories to the Italian press—which is utterly devoid of principle or integrity—and the American papers and news magazines then pick up the story with no more verification than the Italian papers require.

The so-called scandal involving a bank in Milan is seven years old and dates back to the involvement of Michele Sindona, a mysterious Italian financial operator, in Vatican affairs. Archbishop Marcinkus has been routinely blamed by the American media for bringing this character into the Vatican, whereas, in fact, Marcinkus has taken the heat for a decision that was made much higher up in the Vatican—according to James Gollin in his masterful study of Catholic finances, written before the scandal —by Pope Paul VI himself.

The only way Marcinkus can defend himself is to shift the blame upward and he courageously refuses to do that. So his curial enemies, who resent a non-Italian in the bank almost as much as they resent a non-Italian pope, have repeatedly tried to smear him.

And the American media, without any attempt to learn the real facts, continue to go along with the smear.

I would not want Marcinkus for my archbishop any more than I would want him as a foe on the golf course: I would be battered either way. But he deserves a fair shake, and he isn't getting it, in great part because there is so much secrecy that almost any wild accusation is assumed to be true without the need to find proof.

Almost at the same time as the Marcinkus flap, the U.S. Attorney in Chicago declared the accusations against Cardinal John Cody moot. You cannot indict a dead man. The Chicago Catholic paper and the Chancery Office, in a burst of intellectual dishonesty, promptly proclaimed that the cardinal had been posthumously vindicated.

But such claims are hollow. As the Chicago *Tribune*, which pussyfooted through the Catholic crisis in Chicago, tartly noted, "It is not enough for the prosecutor and the archdiocese and the news media to say the case is over. It is not over in the minds of thousands of people who are left wondering about the behavior of their institutions, their government, their churches, their sources of news. The criminal investigation, concluding as it did in an announcement of soaring ambiguity, settled nothing."

My impression is that it is impossible to vindicate the late cardinal without a public audit of the church's finances. Until that happens, there will be widespread suspicion that the cardinal's refusal ever to reply to the charges was a tacit admission of guilt. I hear the people of Chicago that I know saying, if he was innocent, why the cover-up?

I have no way of knowing what the truth is and will not make the judgment that where there was so much smoke there had to be some fire. My criticisms of the late cardinal dealt with other matters. Yet I see the point of the question and I wonder why, if there was nothing to hide, so much was hidden.

The new archbishop, Archbishop Joseph Bernardin, appointed with almost indecent haste as soon as the government mooted the investigation, will bear the legacy of suspicion and distrust he has inherited unless he clears the air with a public revelation of the facts.

I don't know whether he wants to do this or not. But I doubt very much that even if he wanted to he could. Surely he comes to Chicago with orders to cover up the facts, to bury the accusations and the possible scandal as deeply as it can be buried.

That's the way the church operates, and no one in a position of responsibility in the church dares to operate any differently.

Pope Leo XIII once said that the church has nothing to fear from the truth.

It's hard to find any Catholic leaders today who would agree.

Vatican Problems
Are Big News

The Wall Street *Journal*'s recent article on the Vatican is the most candid and detailed report on the administrative and financial problems of the Holy See that I have ever seen in an American paper. It is one more massive piece of evidence of what some of us have been trying to tell church authorities for years: The Vatican Council made the Catholic Church worldwide news. Now scandals in church administration have made the hitherto secret inner workings of the church hot media copy.

When the *Journal*, one of the world's most responsible newspapers, turns its enormous journalistic energies on the Vatican, the Catholic Church is faced with a "sign of the times": It no longer has the luxury of secrecy, it is working in the open, on the rooftops, as the Founder said, whether it wants to or not, whether it thinks it is or not.

The *Journal* article, widely reprinted elsewhere, was generally excellent, save for two inaccuracies that seem incorrigible in American reporters trying to figure out what's happening in the Vatican:

1) The Vatican Bank (The Institute of Religious Works) and the Vatican investment portfolio are not the same operation. The institute does not handle the Vatican's endowment (which is notably less than, let us say, that of the Ford Foundation).

2) Archbishop Paul Marcinkus, the perennial whipping boy of American journalists, did not bring Michele Sidona, who is currently serving a jail term for fraud, into the Vatican, and Sidona did not work out of the bank. Sidona was a protégé of Pope Paul VI.

The *Journal* article, however, did report several important facts that are well enough known by Vatican watchers but which many Catholics are reluctant to admit.

1) The pope is in favor of more openness and accountability in the church's financial administration, though doubtless something less than complete openness and full accountability. He is not yet ready to move everything up on the rooftop. Or if he is, he has not been able to constrain the Roman Curia to financial openness.

2) The pope, for all his wonderful abilities and gifts, is not a very good administrator. He puts off decisions, governs with a small personal staff, ignores the Curia but does not dominate it and lets work pile up on his desk while he travels the world.

All the recent popes have developed techniques for counterbalancing the Curia. Pope John summoned a council; Pope Paul had a chief of staff who chewed the bureaucrats into line;

Pope Pius pretended, in his final years, that they were not there and administered the church with the help of his housekeeper.

John Paul II apparently is following Pius' method—though with a small, mostly Polish staff instead of the housekeeper.

But what might have worked a quarter of a century ago won't work today. The administrative and financial problems of the church are much more serious, and papal administration, once protected in reverent secrecy until a pope was dead, is now subject to instant review in the world press.

Catholics may differ about the desirability of the latter development; however, they are kidding themselves if they think it is a reversible phenomenon.

I am inclined to think that is a good if painful development, another way of saying that the Founder was right about rooftops. Few people could read the *Journal* article and not conclude that the administration of the church needs a profound overhaul, and not merely a cosmetic reorganization and "internationalization" of the sort that has happened a couple of times in the last two decades. Such an overhaul would involve a final and ultimate crushing of the power of the curial bureaucracy—perhaps by making it subservient to a board of residential bishops from around the world.

The focusing of public attention on the sad state of church administration may hasten the day of such a desperately needed reform, a reform that incidentally must assume as a matter of course that the Vatican can no longer keep secrets any better than the White House can.

For the church is now irrevocably on the front page and, like it or not, on the housetops.

YOUTH

For the first five years of my ordained life I was a teenage priest.

The pastor did not trust me with the laity. Not just me, though. He was afraid that his curates would supplant him in the affections of "his" people. So I was turned over to the teens, a group of people about whom I knew nothing, never having been a teenager myself. (The word was invented after I left the teens behind.)

Now some of my teenagers of those days have teens of their own.

And mess up every bit as badly as did their parents.

It makes you wonder.

The most attractive thing about the young is that they have open if shallow minds and are hungry to learn what life means.

And the most unattractive thing is that most of them close their minds at twenty or so and become just like their parents, even though they may wear different clothes, use different words and spout different slang.

I am impressed by how little young people have changed in three decades. Most of the "eras" of which pop social scientists write are either superficial fashions or tendencies among the Harvard-attending elites. Even during the allegedly radical sixties, most young people were not radical. And even during the allegedly stable and conservative fifties, chastity was not all that popular.

So one keeps trying with the young, especially during those few years between sixteen and nineteen when some of them have a sense of wonder.

And you realize that the Omega Point is not right around the corner.

Please Don't Spoil the
Grammar-school Football Season

It's about time for the grammar school football season to start again, and the remnants of my conscience torment me for the contributions I've made to the development of this monstrosity. Grammar school sports are too important to be left in the hands of young priests.

A quarter of a century or so ago, when I showed up in a parish, the eighth-grade football team was a bedraggled, pick-up bunch of kids with tattered uniforms, poor equipment, no coach and a remarkable inability to get the ball across the goal line.

They also had a lot of fun, particularly in their annual Thanksgiving Day classic with the parish to the south of us, not infrequently upsetting the Enemy, who Cheated, of course.

The parents whispered in my ear that wasn't it a shame that a parish like ours didn't have a better-organized program of grammar school sports. Not knowing any better (and desperately loving to win), I agreed. So we found the money (I don't remember how, but I know I didn't steal it), bought equipment, uniforms, hired a coach and even organized a conference of about thirty parishes. We won championship after championship.

I knew we had made a mistake on the Sunday afternoon when the mothers of the kids on our team and the mothers of the kids on the other team (they Cheated, of course) engaged in a hair-pulling brawl that lasted fifteen minutes. It was too late then, however. Like Dr. Frankenstein, I had created my monster.

I think we only spoiled a few lives with our grammar school program, and in retrospect, I suppose those lives would have been spoiled by their parents anyhow. But I certainly didn't impede the spoiling.

I concluded after a few years, and still firmly believe, that the only kind of grammar school sport is one like our girls' volleyball team: Kids organize it, kids run it, kids play it. You do everything you possibly can to discourage parents and other family members from showing up for the games. (Our girls were perennial city volleyball champions. They did not Cheat, of course.)

I might be willing to allow competitive varsity sports for juniors and seniors in high school, though again the football and basketball "club" concept in which the young people organize their own programs is much to be preferred. I don't mind professional sports when they are played by adults (well, I do mind the way professional football is played by the Chicago Bears, but that's another matter), but I don't want professionalism in grammar school, high school or college. I'll let audiences watch college games and maybe, grudgingly, some high school games, but I don't want parents or families or friends or cheerleaders or rooters or anyone else messing up athletics and athletes when they are under sixteen years old.

One parent said to me when I propounded this radical position, "But sports are what life is all about. Life is competitive and you have to learn how to win under pressure."

No way. There is some competition in life, of course, but only one team can be national champions or state champions or city champions. Only one kid can win a golf or tennis tournament. Everyone else is a loser. (If you are in Chicago, that means you lose all the time.) However, in the game of life, one person's winning does not mean other people lose. There can be all kinds of winners. In fact, everybody can be a winner with his/her own talents, gifts, abilities and destiny. You don't have to compete against others nearly so much as you have to compete against yourself. You don't have to win over others. You have to win over yourself. Happiness in marriage, parenting, neighborhood or career does not mean you have to beat someone as you do in a sudden-death overtime in an athletic contest. Competitive sports really aren't a preparation for life; not, at any rate, for those parts of life which are most important.

That is not to say competitive sports are devoid of purpose or function in the human condition. It is merely to say that the purpose and function is best served when competitive sports are carefully limited and placed within a broader context of total human development. Maturation is possible, of course, if you're a winner; Chris Evert Lloyd, in her recent interview with Phil Donahue, made poignantly clear how hard it is.

It really is all right if kids under sixteen win, just so long as their parents aren't around to pull one another's hair after the game is over.

Today's Teens:
Back to the 1940s?

It is one of the clichés of popular journalism that the young people on the college campuses today are much more stable, straight, square, responsible, conservative and concerned about career and security than were their predecessors, the rebel youth of the 1960s or the narcissistic youth of the "me" decade, the 1970s. However, a number of recent surveys of teenagers—those still in high school—lead me to wonder if we are returning not to the fifties but to the late forties, to the years immediately after the end of World War II.

The most striking hint that the future might look like the late 1940s is the emphasis placed on home and family life in the future plans of today's high school students. The young women in particular seem almost innocent of any traits of feminism and are vigorously committed to the importance of being a wife and a mother, as were their grandmothers almost forty years ago.

I do not predict necessarily a return to the baby boom or the reappearance of the suburban domesticity of the "togetherness" years. Yet, I'm struck by how much today's teens resemble the people who went to high school when I was growing up. The big difference, of course, is that we had the Great Depression just behind us and they have Vietnam and Watergate just behind them.

It must be remembered that today's teens grew up in a time when everybody was talking about "limits" of economic growth and the "sickness" of the American economy and the "decline" of America as the world's greatest industrial power. Recent economic indicators suggest that much of that pessimism is unmerited, and indeed quite independent of President Reagan's new economic policy. So it may well be that, relative to what they expect, today's teenagers are going to experience an economic expansion.

Today's teens may be less likely to have to compete for jobs when they emerge from college or professional schools in the middle or late eighties. An unexpected surge in prosperity and their own highly domestic and domesticated values might create a situation reminiscent of that at the end of the Second World War.

I would suggest that there are two explanations that may provide a hint of what's going on:

1) Young people have a remarkably acute ability to perceive the mistakes of their elders. For many of them, the narcissistic radicalism of folks now in their late thirties or early forties may seem ridiculous revolutionary posturing and posing which did not change society and does not seem to make those who grew up in that era particularly happy or particularly successful spouses and parents. So, say our shrewd teenagers, let's be responsible, solid, and seek our comfort and happiness in the joys of family life.

2) It may well be that the middle class—and America is a massively middle-class country—ordinarily and routinely is domestic and respectable in its orientation, and that departures from these norms represent temporary historical aberrations brought on by special conditions. The organizational man in the gray flannel suit of the forties and fifties may be characteristic of most American middle-class young people when conditions permit. Between

1965 and 1975 (roughly), America went through a very peculiar period in its history. The largest age cohort the country ever knew tried desperately to squeeze through an institutional structure that did not have enough room for them, while at the same time the country endured assassinations, riots and disorders at home, a frustrating and destructive war overseas and the gravest scandal in the history of the presidency.

Under such circumstances, young people were willing to listen to the prophets of revolution and narcissism on the college campuses. Now that that era has passed, young people routinely return to those values and attitudes, especially the ones supporting family and home, which had been characteristic of the American middle class. The fundamental difference between generations, then, will depend on whether economic prosperity is considered to be good as it was in the 1950s, or uncertain as it was in the late 1940s.

All this is very speculative. No historical era repeats itself exactly. It is too early to say what values and goals the teenagers of today will finally choose. Moreover, even at the height of the radicalism of the late sixties, most young people were neither radicals nor revolutionaries and wanted basically what their parents wanted—home and family and a career which would support them plus provide some minimum challenge and satisfaction.

You do not have to be a weatherman to know that the winds they are a-changin'.

The End of the Sixties Revolutions?

It was fashionable to proclaim after John Lennon's tragic death that the various "revolutions" of the sixties that his music symbolized would be the most powerful memorial to his life.

Rock 'n' roll music may continue, but the death of Lennon might well be described as a symbol not of the continuity of the values of the sixties (by which are actually meant the years between 1966 and 1974) but of their end.

There are now enough surveys of contemporary teenagers to enable one to say with confidence that many of the values the sixties rejected are back in vogue—chastity, virginity, motherhood, fidelity, family life, privatism, good grooming, personal fulfillment and happiness. Looking at the empirical evidence, one has a twinge of déjà vu—it is not 1980 but 1952.

Moreover, the return to the "old ways" seems especially pronounced among the better-educated young people and among those in their early teens, suggesting we are seeing not a fluke but a trend of some durability.

The young people of the 1980s may change as they grow older, though it is well to remember that the 1950s were not the time of stern moral rectitude that a kind of inverted nostalgia attempts to recall.

Moreover, no two historical segments are strictly comparable. The young of the present are different from those of the Eisenhower years in many ways, not the least of which is that they are choosing more conservative "lifestyle values" because of their own free choice and not because parental values are being imposed on them. Indeed, many of the younger teens are clearly the offspring of the fifties generation, quite deliberately rejecting their parents' values of permissiveness.

No one ought to be surprised by such a change. There are historical rhythms, which no one fully understands, that seem to influence such matters. The "domestic" forties and fifties were preceded by the "permissive" twenties and thirties. Only those who, like the sixties "radicals," thought they were the hinge of history believe that human culture and human behavior can be transformed quickly and definitely.

The word "revolution" was used much too loosely during the last twenty years to describe changes that affected only a small segment of the population or that represented continuities rather than dramatic changes. Only a small number of women were ever willing to give up family and motherhood, for example, even though those who did got all the headlines—in part perhaps because they were writing the headlines.

And even in the 1950s a hefty segment of the female population worked even after marriage and children. The revolution was at most a change in emphasis, in conventional wisdom and in the behavior of cultural and intellectual elites. The "reaction" or "backlash" or "return" is not so much the undoing of a revolution as a change in emphasis, a new kind of conventional wisdom and a change in behavior of some segments of the elite.

It is, nonetheless, extremely important. The almost inevitable conflict between the sixties "radicals" and the eighties "conservatives" may be one of the most important phenomena of this decade—especially since the conservatives will have to work for the radicals.

Never trust anyone under thirty.

The Intolerable Waste of Adolescence

My water-skiing companions this summer were a bunch of fifteen- and sixteen-year-old kids; bright, attractive, witty, young people who were perfectly ready to tolerate a weird clergyman as a water-skiing companion, especially since it was his boat.

They reminded me of the young people I knew when I was in my first years of parish work. They too were filled with hope and promise and bright dreams of a life that stretched out ahead of them. They were intelligent, lively, curious about life, eager to learn and discovering quickly that the way to deal with the odd priest was to needle him. Two decades and more have gone by, but teenagers seem very much the same. Indeed, my water-skiing friends were more like the teenagers of twenty years ago than a lot of adolescents who were around in the intervening decades.

Yet, I came away from the water-skiing fun sad and depressed. Maybe it is true that not only should no one ever be a teenager twice (as sociologist David Riesman remarked long ago); maybe it is also true that no one should ever be a teenage priest twice.

For once you've watched a generation of teenagers grow to the age when they have their own teenagers, you cannot help but be sad when you encounter a new generation of bright, hopeful people with their lives reaching ahead of them. You realize that most of them will not achieve anywhere near the happiness of which they are capable, that they will not do with their lives nearly what they might have and that their hopes and expectations will turn into frustration, bitterness and discouragement. You also know that a few of them are going to mindlessly destroy themselves.

What depresses me more than anything else is the waste. There is so much goodness, so much enthusiasm, so much energy, so much openness, so much curiosity, so much possibility. Some dreams don't come true because it is the nature of life for some dreams not to come true. But other dreams don't come true because opportunities are missed, because enthusiasm is discouraged, because openness is slammed shut and because hope is blighted. The private little hells in which many of the teenagers of two decades ago now live were not imposed by fate. They were the result of free choices, made because of parental or cultural pressures, but still free choices. As the old doggerel put it, "For of all sad words of tongue or pen / the saddest are these: What might have been!" . . . But sadder still / it seems to me / are the words / But it shouldn't oughta be.

One can accept as inevitable, though tragically inevitable, the destruction of youthful enthusiasm by poverty or sickness or injustice or oppression. But when enthusiasm is destroyed in young people who are not poor and who are not sick and who are not oppressed, then the waste is intolerable. To make matters worse, if one stays around long enough, one can see the teenagers of yesteryear making exactly the same mistakes with their own teenagers that their parents made with them. The experience causes one to wonder how much progress humankind has made. We have a long, long way to go before we reach Father Teilhard's Omega Point.

The enthusiasm of adolescents of the late sixties and early seventies was an angry, destructive, self-pitying enthusiasm.

That's gone now. The teenagers of the eighties are very much like the teenagers of the fifties. Their enthusiasm, their hope, their openness, their curiosity are normal natural resources. My water-skiing companions may well need experience, maturity, sophistication, discretion, but we need their enthusiasm. I scream in pain and anger when I realize that, instead, we will destroy it.

Working with Teens Is a Plus

I once wrote a column about a pastor whose first move on taking possession of his new parish was to banish teenagers from the rectory. Such a decision by itself ought to be grounds for his parishioners to file a petition with the diocesan personnel board to replace him. Indeed, my colleagues and I, in our report *Young Catholics* (published for the Knights of Columbus by Sadlier), suggest that failure to minister to the teenagers and young adults of a parish ought to be ipso facto grounds for removal of a pastor—so important is the influence of the parish priest on the religious maturation of the young Catholic. Indeed, second only to the quality of the priest's preaching and his parochial effectiveness is his willingness to work with teenagers.

My colleague William McCready once remarked that the Irish, being a modest race, expect only two things from their clergy: That they stand in the back of the church and talk to them on Sunday morning, and that they be nice to the kids (having, I presume, long ago given up on hearing a good homily). This anticipated our research findings and was certainly vigorously supported by them. Yet working with young people seems in disrepute in most parishes of the country. A youth minister may be hired to deal with teenagers and a director of religious education to try to teach them something about their faith (normally a useless effort in a CCD classroom environment), but few priests seem to want to spend time with young people anymore and virtually none of them want teenagers hanging around the rectory or sitting on the front lawn.

I can't think of very many good reasons for having rectories, but one reason surely is that the rectory is an ideal place for teenagers to congregate. The pastor who ejected the teenagers from the rectory did so in the name of restoring "order" to the parish, apparently assuming that a rectory that was empty was an orderly rectory. Doubtless he argued he was perfectly within his rights with the expulsion. After all, it was his rectory, wasn't it? That's right, fella, it was your money that paid for it and hence you can do anything you want with it.

Mind you, there was no complaint from the parishioners about the teenagers' presence. Most of them were delighted because they knew that the priest took advantage of the informality of teenagers in the rectory and turned it into a perfect, "natural" religious education experience—without the necessity of an intervening director of religious education. A number of young people I know went through this informal rectory experience and their lives are profoundly different as a result. Their younger brothers and sisters are to be denied the same experience because the new pastor—twenty-five years younger than the man he replaced—wants an orderly rectory.

This particular incident is important enough in itself, but it is even more important in what it reveals about the American church's approach to young people: If we can herd them off into a classroom with some paid religious-education director, then we are perfectly delighted to do so, even though empirical evidence indicates that such high school CCD efforts are an utter waste of time.

On the other hand, the empirical evidence indicates that personal contact between the priest and teenagers has tremendous payoff. But we want to have no part of such contact, apparently because teenagers are noisy, messy, pushy, troubling creatures. They are the future, of course, but that's hardly an important consideration when a pastor wants an orderly rectory.

Do Computers Ruin Kids?

All the words in this column will be spelled correctly. I don't mean, general reader, that previous columns have been loaded with misspellings. By the time my prose gets to you, it has been sanitized by a diligent group of gnomes from the University of Notre Dame who will someday rise to the top at Universal Press Syndicate—which is a kind of Notre Dame alumni association.

I mean, rather, that the gnomes won't have any spelling errors to catch in the weeks and months ahead. I now have a computer program that won't let me misspell.

O wondrous invention! All my life I have been misspelling certain words without knowing it. Moment has one *m* in the middle; petulance is spelled with an *a*, not an *e;* liaison has two *i*'s. (All right, that's not a word I use much in my writing.) Commitment has two *t*'s, not three; responsibilities, a word I do know how to spell, will emerge from my word processor with all its required *i*'s.

Mind you, I was one of the better spellers of my generation. I used to take first or second place in all the spelling bees in my class. (Do they have such things still?)

Indeed, I think I may have been an obnoxious little boy about my moments of glory to which I had a strong commitment and displayed a marked petulance when the little girl who was occasionally better at it then I (and with whom I never had a liaison) took her responsibilities so seriously as to beat me in one of those matches.

Nonetheless I had, until the arrival of the Radio Shack word processor dictionary, certain deficiencies as a speller.

No more.

In addition, as an added service, my trusty floppy disk will automatically hyphenate words at the end of the line. Even those of you out there who are perfect spellers—better than I and the black-eyed, black-haired Irish wench who beat me occasionally—will admit that they do not understand the rules for English hyphenation.

God bless Radio Shack, past, present and yet to come.

Aha, say the anti-technology nuts among you, one more case of the computer ruining the education of the young. We are raising a generation of mathematical illiterates who have not memorized the multiplication tables and now we will have a generation of spelling illiterates who depend on machines for their spelling skill. Will your dratted word processor produce term papers and short stories and novels?

Not yet.

I am of a mixed mind. A lot of young people of college age can neither add nor spell. Unlike me (and the black-haired, black-eyed Irish wench who occasionally beat me, I presume), they don't merely mess up an occasional word. They can't spell anything. Deep feelings of inferiority over their lack of spelling skills frighten them, sometimes into paralysis, when they are faced with a test or a term paper. For such folks a program that tells them when a word is misspelled is a gift from heaven. They still have to look the word up in the dictionary, but at least they know that their paper will not appear to be the work of a semi-literate.

And how many of you feel constrained to apologize at the end of a letter for your spelling mistakes?

Spelling rules for English are difficult and confusing, hyphenation rules are impossible. A built-in teacher who tells you when you make a mistake or mechanically puts in the hyphenation marks is an adjunct to basic skills, not a substitute for them. If you haven't been made to commit to memory the fact that 7 times 8 equals 56, it will take you a lot longer to figure this with your jim-dandy calculator, wristwatch and Martian invasions toy. The calculator is useful, however, for multiplying 74 by 82. (My machine says that the answer is 6,068.)

The point is that technologies are getting a bum rap when they are blamed for the failures of young people in the basic skills of civilized human beings. No one, not even the most wild-eyed technologist, would claim seriously that calculators and computers are a substitute for basic skills. It just happens that the new technological gimmicks have appeared on the scene at a time when the educational establishment has abandoned all serious effort to teach kids the basic skills.

Kids can't spell and can't add and can't read, not because of computers and calculators and television, but because of rotten teaching and because the good teachers are too busy filling out forms, going to meetings, appeasing principals, maintaining law and order and defending themselves against the natives to impart the fundamental skills that are supposed to be the reason why we have schools.

The educational enterprise has become an end unto itself, no longer a means for skill development.

Don't blame that on the machines.

Teens Turn More Conservative?

Powerful evidence of the resurgence of traditional family values and aspirations of contemporary teenagers can be found in the Twelfth Annual Survey of High Achievers, conducted by Who's Who Among American High School Students.

The teens who fall into this elite group have always been more traditional than their less-successful contemporaries, though they are not necessarily typical in their attitudes. The important fact to note about their attitudes is not that they reflect in precise proportion what a random sample of the teenage population feels in any given year, but how this group of special young people changes through the years.

Since they have been studied carefully for more than a decade, it is not unreasonable to think that the changes among the teenagers reflect changes occurring in the rest of the adolescent population. The proportions in the two groups might be different, but it is unlikely that the direction of change is different.

A decade ago, 21 percent of the achievers used marijuana and 30 percent favored legalization of the drug. The proportions have fallen to 10 percent in both categories this year.

In 1976, two thirds of the achievers approved of premarital

sex; the proportion is now down to 51 percent. In 1970, 70 percent of them approved of legalized abortion; now the percentage is down to 42 percent. In 1970, almost half approved of living together before marriage; now the rato is down to one fifth.

A fifth rejected traditional marriage in 1970, while a tenth do today. More than three fourths have not had sexual intercourse; 31 percent of those surveyed had had sex in the middle 1970s.

Half expect to have three or more children. Five percent expect to have no children, 4 more percent expect to have only one.

There is no difference between young men and young women in expected family size, support for traditional marriage and opposition to abortion; young women are more likely to oppose premarital sex and less likely to have participated in it. Not exactly radical feminists, these young women.

I don't cite this evidence to prove that there is a massive conservative trend among the successful young people, any more than evidence from the late 1960s would indicate a "sexual revolution," as they called it in those days.

Rather, I am arguing that it was a mistake to forecast the future in the late 1960s and early 1970s on the assumption that the attitudes of young people who grew up in the 1960s represented the wave of the future. The young men and women of the 1960s were not the shape of the world to come, despite their frequent assumption that they were the hinge of history.

Neither are the young people of the 1980s the hinge of anything but the next ten years. Revolutions in human behavior tend to be few and far between. Swings in fashion occur periodically for reasons we only dimly perceive. Those who see these ebbs and flows as revolutions know very little of human nature and very little of human history.

Moreover, even in the 1960s, most young people wanted traditional marriages and even in the 1980s some do not. "Free love," as the new movie *Reds* demonstrates, was not an idea invented in 1965.

The "future shock" myth—the idea that we have gone through a sudden, dramatic and revolutionary change, never before experienced in human history—is both self-serving and self-indulgent.

You can sound profound and sensitive at cocktail parties if you pontificate about change; you sound reactionary, old-fashioned and just plain dumb if you talk about the continuity of human experience.

Yet continuity is more important than change in the human condition. The fact that a segment of the present generation of young adults (older than the teenagers in the achievers study) has given up on traditional marriage is not a sign that traditional marriage is finished. Nor is the rejection of the untraditional "lifestyle" by a considerable proportion of elite young people a sign that it will be abandoned completely.

Beware, in other words, of the expert, even the college-professor expert, who tells a reporter looking for a story that a behavior pattern in which the professor happens to be engaged is the way everyone will live twenty years from now.

As the great social thinker Sportin' Life (in *Porgy and Bess*) would have remarked, "T'ain't necessarily so."

Trading One Group for Another

Young people are likely to become the new scapegoat class in society, the new pariah group everyone may freely and acceptably hate.

We all resent the young because they are young and we are not. Envy is one of the most powerful and most fundamental of all human motivations. In each of us there lurks a strain of envy for those who apparently have longer lives ahead of them than we do.

As the population composition changes, the young will become a relatively smaller and less influential group. It will be easier to speak of our resentment toward them, especially since they will be the working force which will be supporting many of the rest of us at wages which we will think altogether too high.

In addition, we will not find it difficult, indeed do not find it difficult now, to equate all the young with the delinquents, the punks (as in punk rock) and the vicious criminals who are a tiny proportion of their number. The "bad guys" in *A Clockwork Orange* were the young. Anthony Burgess seemed to have uncovered a particularly secret corner of our unconscious with that book and film. It is now much more permissible to speak what we used to harbor in the depths of our angry envious souls about young people.

The old have become faddish. There is money to do research on them; concern about their problems is avant-garde; sympathy for them is fashionable (none of which is to say we have yet begun to treat the old justly).

Indeed, the old seem to have replaced the young as the darlings of the nation's deep thinkers and high-level worriers. Never trust anyone under thirty.

Part of the change can be attributed to the fact that the sixties generation—the most narcissistic, self-centered, self-pitying age cohort the nation has ever known—is now no longer young. Its members are over thirty and almost by definition that means that those under thirty are no good.

I was recently reading a book—an excellent book, by the way—by one of the sixties generation. He remarks that teenagers the world over are "loud, unpleasant, rude." This but a few pages after he bragged about his own proud contribution to the chaos of the Woodstock generation. It's all right when my generation was rude, you see, but wrong when others are.

The sixties crowd is also given to producing articles telling us in shocked horror how the younger generation is no longer interested in "radical" or "idealistic" causes—which means the causes that were popular fifteen years ago—and is concerned only about making money. These articles are written, of course, by high-priced journalists who have become very much a part of the "radical" journalistic establishment. Success, you see once again, is all right when it comes to me and my friends, but it's wrong when those punk kids work for success.

Even the clergy, once the high priests of youth worship, seemed to have tired of them. It's hard to find a young priest or minister who cares about kids any more. The evidence is that teenage and young adult time is critically important to religious development. But the clergy are now seeking relevance somewhere else.

By ministering to old people, they claim.

The Impossible Situation in Our Public Schools

Does anyone think that cities like Cleveland and Chicago would be having school crises if it were not for race? Or to put the matter differently, were there ever any such crises when the majority of students in the urban public schools was white?

If there are financial shortages or cash crises in urban public school systems, the reason is that ultimately the city schools depend on the support of white taxpayers and their representatives in the state legislatures, neither of whom are disposed to pour money into urban public school systems and attempt to educate students, most of whom are black, and to pay teachers, many of whom are black. It costs more money to run an urban public school system than a suburban, partly because teachers' unions are likely to be more militant, partly because the larger the system the bigger the structure of administrative bureaucracy deemed necessary to run it and partly because of the special costs (in vandalism, for example) of trying to educate the urban poor.

If the urban school districts were reorganized to include not only the inner city but also the suburbs and even a substantial chunk of downstate, you just watch the financial crisis in the city schools go away.

The top-level administrators of urban public schools have three impossible tasks. First of all they are expected to educate young people, even though many of the students receive no support or reinforcement or encouragement for educational achievement at home. When such students fail to achieve high scores on standardized tests, it is invariably the administrators (and the city politicians) who are blamed by the press and by community leaders. No one seems to notice that *all* urban public school systems have exactly the same problem, no matter who the school superintendent is or who the mayor is. Blaming the school for the failure of the family is excellent therapy but it is not, however, an intellectually honest discussion of the problem.

The second impossible task of urban public schools is to maintain fiscal stability while caught between militant unions and parsimonious state legislators. Teachers were slow to get into the organizing business but they have made up for lost time. Ironically, the same editorial writers and community "spokespersons" who demand quality education for minority group children oppose the upgrading of teachers' salaries. They never do say how you are supposed to get good education when you pay teachers poorly (I've always been amused by the fact that America pays high salaries to doctors who take care of children's bodies and low salaries to teachers who take care of their minds).

The third dilemma of the school administrators is how to get anything done in a system that is overloaded with an incompetent and unnecessary administrative bureaucracy. The urban Catholic schools have demonstrated for many years that you can run an effective and relatively inexpensive urban school system with virtually no administrative overhead; less than $50 per pupil per year in New York Catholic schools as compared to $1,000 per pupil (at least) in the New York public schools. The dead weight of useless administrative bureaucracies makes change and improvement in the public schools next to impossible, even if there were the money and the family environment to improve the quality of education.

What's the answer?

The answer is that there is no answer; not in the present system of urban public education. Freedom of educational choice is an eventual long-term solution—a voucher system in which control of the schools is taken away from the politicians and the professional educators and given back to the parents, which would smash the public education monopoly and establish a free market in which schools might compete based on the quality of their performance. But the lobbies of professional educators are going to stall that option for a long time yet. The racism of white taxpayers and legislators and the militancy of the teachers' unions will keep the urban public schools chronically ill for a long, long time.

Meanwhile, somebody ought to think of simply turning the public schools over to the Catholic Church. "You folks do such a good job and do it so cheaply," the voter and the taxpayer might say, "that we will let you run our schools too."

The leaders of the church would turn down the offer anyway. They may be pretty dumb but they are not that dumb.

How Religious Are Young People?

In a charming homily inaugurating his term, the new archbishop of Chicago imagined E.T. checking in at the Drake Hotel and then wandering over to Oak Street Beach to inquire of the young people what they thought of the coming of a new archbishop.

The Extra-Terrestrial would be told, observed the archbishop, that religion didn't make much difference to them. They didn't take religion very seriously, though they hadn't left the church. The installation of a new archbishop was something for their parents, who were home watching it on TV, and not for them.

Well, I don't know. The teenagers that I talk to tell me that the new archbishop is "cute," a term normally used for such appealing characters as E.T., Leonard Nimoy and Robert Redford.

More to the point, perhaps, is the fact that, in his new archdiocese this summer, over one thousand young adults participated in a parish-based theology program, administered, incidentally, by an agency whose funds the archbishop's predecessor had cut off.

The picture, then, is complicated—there are the enthusiasts

discussing theology, the indifferents on the beach and the antag-
onists muttering sullenly in the bars that they'd sooner watch the
red-hot Chicago Cubs (a true miracle if there ever was one)
than an archbishop.

And the majority who are none of these. As one of my students in Arizona remarked, "I'm not religious now, but I will be
later when I'm older and have a family and when I'm much
older and know I'm going to die."

"What if you knew you were going to die in six months?
Would you turn deeply religious then?"

"You'd better believe it," she replied.

Thus one must be equally wary of those who comfortably
announce that Youth (with a capital *Y*) are searching for God
and of those who with equal comfort proclaim that Youth is not
interested in God (often adding that Youth will only be interested in God when the churches take the proper stands, that is
to say liberal stands, on political and social issues).

In fact, youth for the most part—and like most everyone
else—puts God on the back burner.

Some young people are God-obsessed, some are angry at
God, some bitterly opposed to religion, some explicitly indif-
ferent. Most hedge their bets, which seems to them the sensible
thing to do.

But the proportions change.

And the empirical evidence that is available to us suggests
that in this particular time, the young people in the Chicago theology program point in the direction in which the steam is
flowing. They are not anything like a majority, but they are
becoming a bigger part of the "mix" of their generation.

We have, in other words, left behind the late sixties and the
early seventies when the balance was shifting in the direction of
anti-religious young people. We are in a new era when there is
probably more authentic interest in religion in the young adult
population than the churches realize.

And certainly more than the Catholic Church is willing to
admit. Young people in Catholicism are almost as second-class
as are women. And to be a young woman is to really rank low
on the ladder.

Even the so-called liberal Catholics are more interested in

the Third World than they are in their own young people—whom they usually denounce as materialistic and devoid of social concern.

And the young women as victims of false consciousness.

If you are a young Catholic woman, you lose on both sides. The conservatives don't want you administering the Eucharist and the liberals resent your domesticity.

If Chicago's new archbishop tries to find out how much of the resources of the diocese are being expended on people like those whom E.T. might interview on Oak Street Beach, he would learn that next to nothing is spent, probably less than the Mass stipends sent to Rome each year.

One of the reasons for the lack of interest is that the church is afraid of the questions young people will ask about sex—a subject on which Catholicism can currently reply, it would seem, only with nervous negatives.

Yet members of the current crop of Catholics turning twenty, the first post-Vatican Council generation, are more conservative sexually precisely because they have more loving and tender images of God.

And this is even more frightening to Catholic leadership. What do you do with young people who are disposed to think of God as lover and a mother?

You do what most other ideological religious leaders of the left or right do: You hope to hell they stay on Oak Street Beach.

THE POPE

The Apostolic Delegate recently sent a secret letter to the American hierarchy warning them of the dangers of my column (though not mentioning it by name) because it was sometimes critical of the Holy Father.

The bishops, said the Curial Careerist, will know their obligations in these matters.

Sure enough, some of them did. The column was dropped by a number of Catholic papers, usually on trumped up grounds and despite the protests of readers.

The cancellation also made many priests—furious that I had begun to write novels which people read—happy.

So much for freedom of expression within the institutional church.

But I don't think these columns are unfair to the pope. On the contrary, they are an attempt to explain his complexity and defend the richness of his teaching. I don't know of any other Catholic writer who has tried so often to interpret and promote the remarkable audience talks the pope has been giving on sexuality, talks which someday will be held to be landmarks in Catholic thought.

But what the Delegate and others like him want is pope-worship. And to worship the pope means you don't tell the truth about his successes and his failures.

The name of the game is not truth. It is idolatry.

And that's how apostolic delegates get to be cardinals.

Another Papal Mistake

Pope John Paul has made an unfortunate blunder in his implied swipe at the church's marriage tribunals (courts) in the United States. It is unfortunate because it is misinformed and aimed at those who are his friends, not his enemies, and it is a blunder because the attack will certainly be counterproductive.

The pope thinks that the number of "annulments" (declarations that a marriage is not "sacramental" and hence not indissoluble) are a threat to the sanctity of marriage. He does not realize, apparently, that there are two reasons for the number of annulments coming from the United States: First of all, American Catholics still care about church law, and secondly, American bishops and priests, pastorally responsive to this concern, have set up the largest and most efficient Catholic marriage courts in the world.

In other words, the pope has attacked those who believe in the law and are interested in serving the good of human souls. In most other countries both priests and people pay little attention to church law or, in countries like Italy where the church still influences civil law, people simply take lovers when a marriage does not work out. I wonder if the pope thinks there is a greater concern for the sanctity of marriage in Italy than in the United States. Is marriage more honored where legal processes are carefully carried out and the pastoral good of souls taken seriously or where it is socially acceptable to practice routine marital infidelity?

Moreover, if he tries to clamp down on ecclesiastical courts who claim they are following both Roman norms and Roman jurisprudence, if he attempts to close down the "annulment" approach, then all that will happen is that American priests will give "internal forum annulments" in the rectory parlors and the process will have become, like so many other things in the Catholic Church, completely out of control.

Nor is there much the pope can do to stop that. His new agent in America, Archbishop Pio Laghi, may try to appoint bishops who will enforce the papal wishes. The only result will be that bishops will be even more isolated from their priests and people than they already are.

The underlying problem is that the American clergy, some American bishops and an increasing number of laity are operating with different theologies with respect to both the church and marriage from those the pope and the Roman Curia accept.

It is worth observing, incidentally, that these theological questions are still open in the sense that there has never been any definitive doctrinal pronouncement on them.

Many American Catholics (and most of the clergy, I believe) do not think the church ought to be in the law business at all. They will go along with the church law as long as the law seems reasonable, but they refuse any longer to think of the church in juridical and legalistic terms. Moreover, they do not see marriage as a contract which becomes an indissoluble sacrament on the day that consent is exchanged. Rather they see it as a commitment between two people which must grow and mature before it becomes a sacrament and hence indissoluble.

Most American Catholics don't know it, but they have history on their side. For most of the first thousand years of Christian history, the church was not in the law business and marriage was a secular event—one with religious implications, no doubt, but not one over which the church exercised any power or for which it had any particular ritual.

Only when civil law collapsed at the time of the barbarian invasions did the church become involved in the law business and in the supervision of marriage, and then only because there was no other authority available.

Moreover, it was only in the sixteenth century that it became a requirement that a marriage occur before a priest and two witnesses, and only in the nineteenth century that Pius IX, in a nondoctrinal statement, equated the contract on the day of marriage with the sacrament and hence with indissolubility.

The pretense of some Catholic conservatives that the way

things are now is the way they have always been will simply not stand up to five minutes of historical investigation.

The annulment process makes sense if a) the church is going to continue to regulate marriage by laws (which it didn't always do and doesn't have to do) and b) one assumes that not everyone is sufficiently mature on the day of marriage to make the kind of long-term, deeply personal commitment that a sacrament is supposed to be.

Neither assumption is in any sense an attack on the sanctity of marriage, and it is unfair and gratuitously uncharitable to attack the priests and bishops who have worked so hard in establishing the system.

Unfortunately, the pope seems to think that a few whirlwind tours of the United States make him an expert on American Catholicism. If he does not drop that notion, he is going to make more and worse blunders.

Papacy a "So-so Job"

On the plane ride home from Anchorage, Alaska, Pope John Paul told reporters who asked him how he liked his job that it was only "così-così"—an Italian phrase which is translated inadequately as "so-so" (it is usually spoken with a resigned wave of the hands). It was not exactly a ringing endorsement of the joys of being a pope in the modern world.

It has not been an easy time for the Polish pope. Like his predecessor, he is intent on restoring order in the church. He wants a careful, guided development of the insights of the Second Vatican Council. Like his predecessor, he does not seem to know quite how to recapture the order of the past. Like his predecessor, he does not seem capable of dramatic and decisive acts of repression that would restore order at the enormous cost of massive defections—the sort of decision that would not have bothered most of the popes called Pius one bit.

Consider the rebuffs to his call for order in the past two

years. He visited Latin America and warned priests and nuns to
stay out of direct political action. Currently the quasi-Marxist
government in Nicaragua is served enthusiastically by the local
clergy, and the Marxist revolution in El Salvador has the ardent
support of militant priests and nuns.

He visited the United States and told the clergy and laity
that birth control was wrong. The people cheered and kept right
on practicing birth control. He warned against the dangers of
hasty marriage annulments. The various diocesan tribunals
around the country agreed completely that hasty annulments
were a bad thing, denied that theirs were hasty and went on
about their business.

He summoned the Dutch bishops to Rome and sternly ordered them to straighten out the mess in the church in their
country. They returned to Holland, did their best (though with
some lack of enthusiasm), and were able to change very little
because the clergy and the laity rejected the pope's right to in-
terfere in their work.

He intimidated the bishops of the world at their synod in
Rome so that there was no frank discussion of the erosion of the
church's credibility in sexual teaching. The bishops issued harm-
less reaffirmations of traditional teaching in traditional formulas.
No one listened. Many of the bishops, including the Americans,
had to return home sheepishly and try to offer lame explanations
to their people as to why they were not more forthright.

On his Asian trip he once again warned priests and nuns to
stay out of political action. Even before he boarded the plane
for the flight to Japan, it was obvious that they would not obey
him.

The pope's campaign to restore order in the church seems to
be taken more seriously by the secular press than it has been by
Catholics. Laity, clergy, even bishops are so preoccupied with
their day-to-day responsibilities and problems that they have little time or inclination to attend to abstract papal pronounce-
ments that do not seem pertinent to our understanding of their
difficulties and predicaments.

Does John Paul know that very few are listening to what he
says, no matter how much they may cheer for his person? The
Roman Curia surely will not tell him the truth, neither will the

sycophants in the papal diplomatic service. Neither will the bishops who at the synod showed they had only enough hormones to tell the pope what he wanted to hear. Yet John Paul is a most intelligent man. He probably knows that there are problems of credibility, though he may not know how acute they are.

His campaign to restore order thus far has two major accomplishments: Hans Küng and Robert Drinan have lost their jobs. Presumably the pope had more than that in mind.

Orders from Rome have routinely been disregarded in the history of the church. In ages past, when transportation and communication were inefficient, the pope did not even try to exercise worldwide control. Recent attempts to do so have been successful in some countries like the United States but rather unsuccessful in other countries like France or Italy. There are two new aspects to the current inattention to the pope: 1) It is to be found even among the most devout and dedicated Catholics; 2) It is open and public, not secret and hidden. Small wonder that John Paul does not like his job.

Papa Wojtyla is the most gifted man to sit on the throne of the Fisherman in centuries. The critical question now is whether his gifts include the ability to admit that he has made a strategic mistake. The world is not Poland. Church orders are not routinely obeyed anymore (if they ever were). You do not tell people what to do before you have won their confidence and their credibility. To do that you must first listen to what they are saying and understand their needs and problems.

The goal of more order in the church is a praiseworthy one. The pope will only achieve it, however, when he is perceived as comprehending that the reasons for the disorder and the confusion are not to be found in perversity, disobedience or infidelity but rather in the genuine religious needs and aspirations of the Catholic people to which the institutional church—and especially the Roman Curia—has been completely insensitive for most of this century.

The Dramatic Papacy
of John Paul II

Two and a half years does not provide enough time to make a full evaluation of the dramatic pastorate of Pope John Paul II. It is certainly possible even now to say that just like his predecessor, who lived only thirty days after election, the second John Paul has changed forever the style of the papacy. The Catholic Church will never be quite the same precisely because Karol Wojtyla—poet, philosopher, professor, musician, actor—has sat on the chair of Peter the Fisherman.

John Paul II has been, from the first moment he emerged on the balcony of St. Peter's to speak in excellent Italian to the people of the city of Rome, a charismatic and attractive person. He is a mass-media figure par excellence. Never again will the church dare to elect a pope who at least does not have some kind of public presence.

John Paul has made a deep impression on people all over the world, especially in his native Poland, where the boost to national self-esteem that came from his election has played no small part in the self-confidence of the extraordinary Polish workers' revolution.

But beyond Poland, everywhere in the world the public figure of John Paul kissing children, wearing hats or waving to the people from automobiles has given Catholics new confidence in their church. He has also given non-Catholics new respect or at least new bafflement at this strange human institution, the oldest human institution in the world, but one which seems to have within it enormous capabilities for rejuvenation and renewal.

So one can certainly say at this stage in John Paul's career that he has had a great impact on the papacy and, as a public figure, a great impact on the Catholic image around the world.

However, in terms of the internal workings of the church, it is much more difficult to evaluate the impact of John Paul II. One can fairly say that he has spent much of the last two years learning the job. He didn't have to learn to be a public person. But he has had to learn how to administer this ancient, turbulent and complex institution.

Those who are close to the operation of the Vatican say that he has by no means yet shaped the Roman Curia so it is an effective tool to carry out his wishes. They also say that some of the day-to-day paperwork of the papacy has suffered, because the pope would much rather be out with people than sit at his desk signing documents. He has, according to many Catholics at any rate, made some serious mistakes—mostly because of bad advice that he has received from his staff.

The punishment of the Swiss theologian Hans Küng and the persecution of the Dutch theologian Edward Schillebeeckx have made many Catholics wonder whether there is still any intellectual freedom in the church. The pope's perceived public stands on matters of sexuality and of women's rights have not satisfied many Catholic women and have offended many others.

The actual words of John Paul are normally far more sophisticated and nuanced than the quotations attributed to him in the press. Indeed, it is safe to say that when any expression of his seems to lack qualification or nuance, it is not an accurate reflection of what he has said. Unfortunately, in the world of mass communications, the subtleties get lost.

And so the pope has appeared, sometimes offensively to many Catholics in the world, to be far more conservative than in fact he actually is. The audience talks he has given on Wednesdays (and he was apparently on his way to an audience talk when he was shot) have been a dramatic break with Catholic sexual theories of the past. For almost a year and a half now, every Wednesday, he has reflected on the meaning of human sexuality in his own, sometimes obscure, convoluted phenomenological style. But read carefully, those audience talks are an innovation in Catholic sexual ethics because they shift sharply from legalism to personalism. One of the more conservative members of the Curia is said to have remarked, "Thank God nobody understands those talks, because they are so revolutionary."

In short, one has a hard time trying to evaluate exactly what's going on in the internal administrative affairs of the church in John Paul II's pastorate. There are signs that he is an open, progressive man who is ready to listen, but also signs that he is a staunch, traditional conservative. Probably the best evaluation is to say that he is a man who keeps his own counsel, makes his own decisions and is still in the process of learning his job.

Many have said that it was his intention to do two things in the beginning of his pastorate. The first was to bring the papacy to the world; the second, to harmonize tradition and modernity in the church by restoring some sense of order. The first effort has been successful. The pope has indeed brought the papacy to the world—as it turns out now, at the risk of his life.

The attempt to restore order has been much less successful. He went to Latin America and urged priests and nuns to stay out of politics. They cheered for him and continued to be active in politics. He came to the United States and reaffirmed somewhat cautiously the traditional birth control teaching. American Catholics cheered enthusiastically for him and kept right on practicing birth control. He summoned the Dutch bishops to Rome and instructed them to straighten out the confusion in the Dutch church. The Dutch bishops went home and did their best, but clearly they did not have the power to change the minds of Dutch Catholics. He went to Africa and warned against the dangers of too much Africanization in the church. The people cheered for him and the Africanization continued.

Thus, it would appear that the attempt to restore order, at least by giving instructions and laying down rules and commands, simply has not worked. Another strategy will be necessary to restore some sense of stability in the turbulent, restless, dynamic but very alive Roman Catholic Church.

This Complex Pope
Not Easily Pigeonholed

When the Roman inquisitors are finished with the Swiss and Dutch theologians, there is another popular Catholic teacher against whom they ought to take action. This man may well be the most dangerous of all. In a recent talk to tens of thousands of people he spoke of the human experience of nakedness and what it reveals about our nature. Can you imagine the harm such a talk would do to the faithful?

He was talking about the Book of Genesis. He endorsed the very liberal position that the author of the book is not talking about experiences which are "distant in time" but "basic in significance." He added, "The important thing is not that these experiences belong to man's prehistory, but that they are always at the root of every human experience."

Worse still, he argues that when the Genesis author speaks of human nakedness, he is dealing with our basic experience of being persons with bodies that are sexual and indeed male and female combined, "the experience on the part of man of the femininity that is revealed in the nakedness of the body and reciprocally the similar experience of masculinity on the part of the woman."

In the experience of shame, he goes on to say, we have a "liminal" experience of the unity of human nature as male and female. The negative implications of shame are the result of sinfulness; we become "ashamed" of our incompleteness vis-à-vis the other because of our fear and insecurity, but we also perceive, however dimly, that beyond this "ashamedness" there is fundamental truth about the mixture of femininity and masculinity not only in the human species but in each individual human.

It almost sounds as if the man was deliberately propounding feminist propaganda about androgyny. To make matters worse, in his public lectures on these delicate matters, which ought to be more appropriately treated in the rectory parlor or the confessional, he has on occasion cited Sigmund Freud in his footnotes.

I trust that the Congregation for the Doctrine of the Faith will go after him. They won't have to look very far—over to the audience hall where Pope John Paul II speaks every Wednesday morning.

A pope who speaks about the religious significance of nakedness and cites Freud? What's happening to the Catholic Church?

I'm being ironic, obviously. There are, however, a number of important observations that need to be made:

1) Whatever the current difficulties may be between the pope and some theologians (and I think the pope has made errors in judgment), he simply cannot be written off as a traditionalist. Such interpretation of Genesis would have led to his condemnation by the curial authorities twenty years ago and must bother a fair number of them even now—if they read what he says. John Paul is a complex, intricate man. There are strains of traditionalism but also powerful strains of modernity and liberalism.

2) The virtual unanimity of the press accounts describing the pope as "tightening up" or "clamping down" or even "restoring the old church" are at best inadequate and incomplete and at worst downright maliciously bad reporting.

3) The journalists covering Rome and Catholic affairs are intolerably lazy. I know about the papal commentary on the Book of Genesis (he seems obviously to be writing a book while he is pope and trying the book out on his Wednesday crowds) not because I have any secret Roman sources but because I read very carefully the weekly air-mail edition of *Osservatore Romano*. While this journal is about as open-minded as *Pravda*, it has to

print what the pope says (though on occasion it has tried to edit him). I daresay there has never been a serious and sensitive discussion of the human experience of nakedness in its pages before.

Nor can I imagine why a pope's rather startling comments on this endlessly fascinating matter might not be news. The pope is hardly advocating immodesty, but he does talk about the human body in a way which most Catholic priests would not yet dare. I must conclude that a lot of the journalists are at best skimming, if they read such comments at all.

My sense of the situation is that the pope is quite properly concerned when scholars seem to be denying the divinity of Jesus and the resurrection. Make no mistake about it, some people are—they even teach freshmen religion classes at American Catholic colleges (where the students laugh at them). I think he's listened to envious rivals, however, about certain European thinkers whose terminology may be different but whose faith is the same as his. Finally, I think that if he should step down as pope, he'd be in trouble for saying some of the things he does every Wednesday morning.

Accepting the Contradictions of John Paul

Let's suppose that the pope took the following stand:

1) A woman's place is in the home, taking care of her children.

2) The Gospels prevent us from considering the ordination of women.

3) Therefore, because of God's law, we will not ordain women in the Catholic Church.

This is, in fact, what many woman believe he said while he was in the United States. It is a perfectly consistent and coherent position, if unacceptable to feminists. It assumes that women are not equal to men, not at least as far as rights in the occupational and political world.

But in the interview he gave recently to the *Ladies' Home Journal*, the pope said none of these things. Rather he said that:

1) Women have the right to complete equality in the occupational world. They should fight for this equality. If they need help to obtain it, the pope will be glad to help them.

2) The non-ordination of women is not a matter of dogma but a matter of ecclesiastical law.

3) He does not foresee the ordination of women because it would be a departure from the Catholic tradition as officially interpreted by the church.

To many people those positions will seem inconsistent. On matters of the occupational, political and social world the pope sounds like a radical feminist. Inside the church he sounds like an old-fashioned traditionalist. Nor does he fall back on the "God's will" argument to defend his traditionalism. He admits that the non-ordination of women is not a matter of doctrine.

How can one explain the inconsistency? One must presume that the two positions do not seem inconsistent to John Paul. He is one of the most gifted and brilliant leaders of our century. Yet he does not grasp that there is a problem in his stands—not even to the extent of sensing that he must at least appear to explain the apparent contradition of his convictions.

The difficulty seems to run through other aspects of his response to contemporary Catholicism. He brilliantly defends human rights, and yet is not appalled when one of the judges in a heresy trial of a distinguished theologian announces on radio several days before the trial that the man is guilty. Similarly, the day he yielded to the demands of the German cardinals and condemned Hans Küng for theological teachings which Küng says are not his, he also issued a "world peace" statement in which he deplored the distortion of the positions of those who disagree with us. Obviously the pope has reconciled in his own mind such seeming contradictions, but they baffle most of the rest of the world.

Who is the real John Paul—the radical feminist or the ecclesiastical traditionalist? The fierce and passionate defender of human rights or the defender of high-handed authoritarianism in the church?

It would appear that the real John Paul is both. I'm prepared to agree with those who see the explanation in the situation of the church in Poland. Perhaps in a garrison you don't apply your principles to your own organization. With the enemy at the gate, self-criticism may seem a luxury you can't afford.

I hope the bishops in the Western world tell him that he appears horrendously inconsistent to their people. Until then, I insist that the complexity of John Paul must be accepted in its fullness. One cannot pretend that he will ordain women. In this respect he is different from none of his predecessors.

But neither can one deny he has spoken the most radical words in defense of the full equality of women of any pope in history. In this respect he represents the beginning of a new era.

To overlook the ecclesiastical traditionalist would be naive. Few are likely to do that just now. To overlook the radical feminist would be dishonest. For reasons of their own a lot of people are doing that. In the long run the radical John Paul will be the one who shapes Catholic history . . . Maybe eventually he will convert the traditional John Paul.

Till then, we will have to live with the complexities and the contradictions.

The Pope on the Family
—Again

"Has your friend the pope gone bonkers?" I was asked recently.

The subject was the new document on the family, summarizing the discussions of the world meeting of bishops a year ago. Or rather the subject was the garbled press reports of the document.

By now the answer is so automatic, I can push a button and it plays itself. The quotes are taken out of context. John Paul is a complex and subtle thinker. He cannot be adequately reported in a few lines. There is much that is positive in the document. It must be read in its entirety. The world media are at fault for not doing a better journalistic job in covering his statements. The Vatican is at fault for not understanding how much papal credibility is harmed by its poor press relations.

I could add that the section of the letter on the rights of women ought to convince feminists that the pope is on their side on most issues. They won't be convinced, because they have already made up their minds on him and because they won't read the document anyway.

Most Catholics won't read it.

Most Catholic priests won't read it.

Most bishops will claim they read it, but I bet they won't.

And that's the real problem—few are listening to John Paul on sex and the family, in part because they don't understand what he is saying.

And much of the reason for the problem is the fact that the pope and his advisers are not listening, either.

They are not listening to what Catholic reporters and journalists say about the necessity for clarity and the danger of the pope being quoted out of context.

The other day, the pope said something such as there was

no marriage in heaven, and the world press was in an uproar.
What he actually said was that when Jesus said there was no
marriage in heaven, he did not mean that we cease to be sexual
beings in heaven—exactly the opposite of what he was reported
as meaning.

After a while, you have to lay the blame right at the papal
doorstep for such misunderstandings. The pope must be clearer
and more concise in his statements or he deserves to be misunderstood and the dodos at the Vatican press office should foresee
and prevent this, instead of trying to correct the misunderstanding when it's too late. (Anticipating mistakes instead of
responding to them could hurt your ecclesiastical career, which
is all the Vatican press people care about.)

The harsh judgment the pope made about the quality of the
marriage relationship between spouses who practice birth control is a philosophical judgment and not a psychological one. Yet
that does not appear in the press quotes of what he said, and
many Catholic laity are profoundly offended, demanding to
know how the pope can make such a judgment about an individual marriage.

So it goes. The Vatican won't listen. Maybe it can't listen.
Too bad then, no one will listen to it.

The inability to listen is made especially clear in the pope's
comment that moral right is not determined by majority opinion,
a cliché tossed around recklessly at the bishops' meeting last
year.

Some journalists saw this as a shot at the United States,
where surveys show that most Catholics reject the pope's teaching on birth control. Actually, surveys show this all over the
Catholic world. The American hierarchy—in a rare moment of
candor—reported the facts of their own situation, telling the
pope what he needed to know instead of what they thought he
wanted to hear.

For those of us who have conducted such surveys, the pope
is at least tacitly implying that we are not crooks and fakers and
that the laity do not go along with his teaching.

But he misunderstands us—probably because he has not
read us and certainly because he does not listen to us—if he

thinks we are arguing that moral right is decided by majority opinion.

No one thinks that to be the case. The position is more moderate, though apparently so subtle as to escape episcopal and papal comprehension: Catholics' experience with marital sexuality ought to be listened to. No more than that. If the laity think the church misunderstands completely what sex means in marriage, ought not the church listen to what they have to say?

And if scientists say that the dimensions of sexuality distinguishing humans from animals reinforce the pair bond between a man and a woman and are not specifically designed for procreation, ought not the pope listen to what these scientists have to say?

The answers to both these questions seem to be no.

It's a shame. He who does not listen will not be listened to —even when the pope has something to say that is extremely important.

AND A FEW
OTHER THINGS BESIDES

What makes you think people care what you think?

Such is a frequent question from priests.

My answer is that I can't imagine why anyone would care what I think.

But I like to write columns and others seem to like to read them. As long as both conditions continue and God continues to give me life and health, I shall continue to say what I think, no matter who it offends.

I will remain both a priest and a writer. I can be thrown out of papers, but I won't leave the priesthood, even if they try to throw me out for saying what I think.

And I am grateful to Monsignor George Higgins, who first suggested I write a column, to Don Quinn, who proposed a regular column, to the late Jim Andrews, who suggested that I try to write for the secular press, to John McMeel, Donna Martin, Lee Salem and Jake Morrissey of Universal Press Syndicate, to Pat Kossmann of Doubleday, who suggested this collection, to Virginia Quinn Reich, Mary Kotecki and Karen Sussan, who typed many of them and to the editors who have the sense to carry the column (alas, none of them in Chicago).

And especially to the readers, whether they agree or not!

St. Patrick's Day Drunkenness

She was thirteen years old and pretty—the pale light skin and dark hair of the black Irish. She was also very drunk, waving a whiskey bottle at the passing traffic on one of midtown Manhattan's busy streets. She was one of the fourth or fifth generation Irish princesses celebrating St. Patrick's Day.

For this did the Wild Geese fly?

One of my friends was not in his office on St. Patrick's Day. When I reached him the following day, I chided him about being afraid to come to New York City on the feast day of the patron saint of Erin. "It wasn't coming to the city that worried me," he said, "it was riding back to Westchester County on the train after the parade."

"You mean those drunken kids were from Westchester County Irish Catholic families?" I exclaimed.

"Of course they were. Not many Irish live in Manhattan anymore."

"What were their parents thinking about?" I demanded.

"They were probably thinking about how they were going to get splendidly drunk that night," he replied ruefully.

I would like to say that St. Patrick's Day drunkenness has nothing to do with being Irish. Unfortunately it has a lot to do with being Irish. It represents one painfully sad aspect of the Irish American experience. In Ireland the pubs are closed on St. Patrick's Day, and the per capita consumption of the "crayture" is less than it is among Irish Americans (sixth of the nine Common Market countries).

Consuming huge amounts of drink, as sociologist Richard Stivers has shown, is an Irish American reaction to the stereotype of the Irish as the stupid and brutal drunk that greeted the

Irish immigrants when they came to this country. As most stereo-
typed populations do, the Irish reacted by accepting the stereotype and converting it into an apparently positive interpretation.
The Irishman, they said, is not a stupid and brutal drunk; he is a
happy, carefree, celebrating drunk.

Like my little friend with the whiskey bottle in midtown
Manhattan.

All subcultures have weaknesses, and there may be worse
things in the world than St. Patrick's Day bashes. Presumably
the black-haired, blue-eyed colleen is sober every other day of
the year. However, there is just enough chance of her being a
confirmed alcoholic by her seventeenth birthday to scare the living daylights out of me. One very famous Catholic women's college has an extensive AA program for incoming freshmen. I am
told that it is necessary and it works quite well.

The problem of alcohol in the early teens is neither a
unique Irish nor a unique St. Patrick's Day problem. Heavy
drinking among junior high school students is approaching epidemic proportions in this country. The young woman shaking
her whiskey bottle at passing taxicabs was the tip of the iceberg,
an iceberg that involves a lot of other youngsters who are by no
means Celtic in their origins.

I am not one of those who believe that the American family
is falling apart. It may in some ways be weaker than it was in
the past; it is surely in some ways stronger as well. It has new
problems, but it also has new possibilities. Yet I am astonished
that American middle- and upper-middle-class fathers and
mothers seem utterly incapable of monitoring the alcohol consumption of young people twelve, thirteen and fourteen years
old. Often the very parents who grow pale with terror at the
mention of the possibility of drug usage among teenagers manage to be serenely oblivious to the fact that alcohol is a far more
serious adolescent problem than marijuana.

Parents of heavily drinking junior high school students deliberately blind themselves to the problem, either because they
do not want to see it or because they do not know what to do if
they admit to themselves that the problem exists. I doubt that
Saint Patrick is pleased with the fact that in his honor young

men and women who are little more than children become disgustingly drunk. On the contrary, I think the good saint must feel very sad—sad for Irish Americans and sad for all American parents who have lost control of their children's lives.

The Scariest Time
of the Year

When I was in high school one of my classmates, now a bishop, used to dress on Halloween with a long, green coat and a green beret and clutch a huge cane in his hand. When trick-or-treaters came to the door he would scream at them in angry German. The only thing he knew in German was the "Our Father." As he said, that scared the kids as much as anything else. The technique was instantly successful. Screaming toddlers, brats and kids would dash down the stairs of his house and flee in panic. The tricksters had been tricked.

"It is a good work," my classmate explained, "for it is much more fun on Halloween to be scared than to scare."

Even then he displayed the wisdom required of a bishop.

Halloween is one of the oldest feasts that humans keep, reaching far back into Celtic antiquity, and even beyond that into the origins of the Indo-European culture and people thousands of years ago. The Celts believed transitions were dangerous times because at times of change the other world, the "many colored lands," interpenetrated with our own. Sunrise, sunset, the changing of the season, changing of states in life were anxiety-producing times, for the fairies were likely to be about at such times and up to no good.

The end of October was an especially dangerous time, for in many of the Celtic lands the transition from summer to winter seemed to occur at this midpoint in autumn. The days were growing shorter, the weather was becoming grayer and colder, the transition to winter was occurring and the fairy-folk were abroad making trouble. The wise person got back to his cottage before it turned dark on such days.

Not only were the fairy-folk out at Samnaintide, as the feast was called in those days. So, too, were many of the ghosts of the dead, not yet freed from this world and not yet accepted into the "land of promise in the West" (the Celtic afterlife). These uneasy dead could not find happiness in the land of promise (which, incidentally, is where Saint Brendan was sailing to when he discovered North America) until they had finished their work on earth—work that often involved avenging wrongs that had been done to them, including, quite often, their deaths. Since the restless dead were often not too discriminating, there was a fair chance that they would confuse you with the person with which they had a score to settle. Both the fairy-folk and the dead were abroad during Samnaintide and ordinary humans were well advised to keep out of their way.

Christianity tried with some success to "baptize" the feast. The restless dead became the souls of purgatory, many of whom were to be admitted into heaven at the Feast of All the Saints (or All Hallows). If there was anybody abroad stirring up trouble on All Hallows' Eve, it was these "holy souls" pleading through prayers that might make it before the final cut on the Feast of All the Saints.

The fairy-folk and the restless dead became the holy souls, and they in turn became the trick-or-treaters. One should not think that turning Halloween from scary terror into scary joke would be foreign to the ancient tradition. The Celts, like the Indo-Europeans who were the ancestors of most of us, thought that there were two ways to deal with the scary folk from the Other World. One was to run in terror from them, and the other was to laugh at them. With fine impartiality, the Celts practiced both techniques interchangeably and simultaneously.

The Irish wake, a strange combination of the terror of death and laughter at it, is a prehistoric custom that represents quintessentially a mixture of terror and laughter in the Celtic response to the fairy-folk and the restless dead and even death itself. Hence, parties, celebrations and even "tricks-and-treats" have been part of the Samnaintide celebration as far back as we can trace it.

The young demons pounding on your doors demanding "good junks" represent a tradition that is as old as history. They are laughing at death and inviting us to laugh, too. Pagan custom or not, it may not, after all, be such a bad idea.

What Christmas Spirit?

It's a shame that Christmas has to come during the holidays.

Instead of putting Christ back into Christmas or, maybe better, taking him out of Christmas, I propose we take Christmas out of the holidays. Let's separate the feast of light and peace and joy, of hope and life, from the frantic, anxious, dehumanizing treadmill of our midwinter holiday festival.

On this happy Sunday a notable portion of the American population (a majority of American women) are in a state of frenzy. Christmas is but a week and a half away, and they are at least two weeks behind in their Christmas preparations. Despite the resolutions made a month ago (and every year made a month ago), the shopping is not finished, the cards are not mailed, the tree is not purchased, the gifts are not wrapped, the invitations have not been sent and the plans of moving from responsibility to responsibility on Christmas Day have not been finalized. What's more, as they anxiously contemplate the time remaining, Americans (and especially American women) know that the frenzy will soon be replaced by despair and the despair by anger, and in all likelihood on the day before Christmas Eve they will come down with a cold.

The problem is especially acute for women because one of the great injustices of our patriarchal male-chauvinist society is to consign to women the responsibility for festivities and celebration and especially the responsibility for Christmas. There may be an occasional man or, even more, an occasional husband, who does some Christmas shopping, but equity in sharing the burden of the awesome Christmas shopping responsibility is so unthinkable as to be beyond discussion. Women do Christmas shopping, don't they? That's what they are for, isn't it?

If you are a person of faith, the deterioration of Christmastime into a frenzy of obligations and responsibilities has to appall you, but even if you are a certified card-carrying agnostic, you must have melancholy moments when you think of how little enjoyment or pleasure or relaxation or happiness is left in our midwinter bash. It all started out as a great idea, but somehow, somewhere, it went wrong.

The nineteenth-century New England descendants of the Puritans tried to eliminate the popish feast of Christmas by creating a rival in Thanksgiving. Indeed, in Massachusetts in the 1870s, the public schools were open on Christmas Day. The papists finally won the contest (took over Thanksgiving for their own too, as far as that goes), and their feast of Christmas is now a certified American festival day. It does not, I think, make the papists especially happy, however, for they too have fallen behind in their Christmas shopping.

The Christmas frenzy is a symptom of a much deeper malaise affecting Americans from the middle class up—chronic inability to control the use of time. Even though we may be the most leisured society that humans have ever known, we have very little leisure. We fill up our nonworking hours with commitments, responsibilities, obligations and compulsions that are as demanding as the work by which we earn our living. If leisure means freedom, then nonworking time certainly isn't leisure, at least for most of us. We have surrounded ourselves with "shoulds," "musts," "have to's," "what will people think if we don'ts." To rephrase C. Northcote Parkinson, "Obligations expand to fill up the time available." No, that's not strong enough. Maybe it should be phrased, "Obligations expand to 1.3 times the time available."

Or let me put it this way, gentlepersons. Who of you that have taken off time to read this column—and feel slightly quilty even about that—does not feel "overcommitted?"

What happens to a society when almost everybody is overcommitted?

It goes mad, of course, only everybody is too busy to know

it has gone mad. As science-fiction writer R. A. Lafferty says in one of his *Apocalypses:* "And then the world came to an end, only everyone was too busy to notice, so they went right on doing what they always did."

I don't know what the solution to the chronic overextension of our time resources is. It is a profoundly important spiritual and human problem, however, and has a pernicious effect on human relationships. If you spend all your time rushing around to fulfill your obligations, you don't have time to love.

As soon as I get caught up on my Christmas shopping, however, I am going to try to find some time to think about this problem.

'Tis the Season to Be Sad

A considerable proportion of the American population goes into an annual holiday funk between mid-December and January 2. Family quarrels, suicides, heart attacks and interludes of psychotic depression increase dramatically all over our republic.

Moreover, many folks, not driven to such extremes, experience blue meanies worse than at any other time of the year.

For some of us, this is the joyous season. For others, it is the sorry season, a time of regret, guilt, self-pity and deep melancholy. How come?

Christmas is, after all, the feast of the light, the celebration of the triumph of day over night, of forgiveness over sin, of life over death. How can anyone look at the crib scene and feel depressed? Why does a day of hope produce sentiments of despair?

There are a lot of reasons, many of them having to do with the less-than-perfect condition of family life. We remember the Christmases of childhood and either regret the passing of their warmth and joy or remember with sadness and guilt their pain. All the family frustrations of our youth come swirling back and we re-enact with our present family or intimate role opposites the conflicts of childhood.

Worse still, we may have to go to Christmas parties with members of our original family in which the old wounds are reopened again. Indeed the wounds are already open when we gather round the tree. Everyone is carefully nurturing the injuries of the past—real or imagined—in the perverse hope that the battles can be fought again. "If they are going to ruin my Christmas, then I'll ruin theirs."

Christmas is a family feast. If one is either isolated from any meaningful family or, worse, caught in old family conflicts, there is little emotional time or energy to look at the family scene in Bethlehem.

Nor does anyone seem to have figured out a strategy for dealing with these problems. Few of us can do what we want at Christmastime. For family means obligations, and a family feast is a feast of obligations. It's often hard to have any fun when you're touching base with all your obligations.

The deepest problem with Christmas, however, is that we're not children anymore. If you're a kid, Christmas is easy: It is a feast of wonder and surprise, of presents heaped up under a tree, of excitement and expectation, of sugar plums and reindeer and then a sleep of healthy exhaustion. We all mourn for the loss of our childhood innocence. At no time is the loss more obvious than at Christmas.

Yet finally, if Bethlehem means anything at all, it is an invitation to return to childhood wonder. The crib scene tells us in effect that whoever is responsible for gifts makes Santa look like a piker (or the minor saint that he really is, Virginia). The trouble with childhood wonder—according to the essence of the Christmas story—is not that it's naive but that it is not wondrous enough. Kids underestimate the grounds for wonder.

Older doesn't necessarily mean wiser. It often means merely more cynical and more disillusioned—that kind of disillusion which, if persisted in (pace T. S. Eliot), is the ultimate illusion.

Christmas then is a battlefield in each of our personalities in which wonder wars with disillusion. If our neuroses are not too strong, wonder still has a fighting chance.

It is Christmas Eve midnight. The tree is lit, the candle is burning in the window. Who can tell whether visitors may be coming?

The Musings of a Modern Traveler

Some random melancholy impressions after having expiated for some of my sinfulness by visiting twenty American cities in twenty days:

1) American ingenuity has developed the finest airplanes in the world, elegant aluminum cylinders that can carry hundreds of people across the continent at more than six hundred miles per hour. Unfortunately, American ingenuity has not discovered how to board these planes. The normal process is for a young person to stand in the doorway and to separate two pieces of paper from each other by tearing them, pieces of paper many of the passengers must fiddle in purses or pockets to find. If a flight is full, there is no way that this poor young person can separate two pieces of paper with enough dispatch to board the passengers so that the plane can leave on time. All heavily booked flights, in other words, are necessarily late because of the problem of separating the two pieces of paper.

Moreover, the airlines have yet to comprehend that passengers are most reluctant to check their luggage, in part because the airlines so often lose checked luggage; thus, they attempt to carry their luggage onto the plane. In half-hearted response to this phenomenon, the airlines provided luggage containers at the front of the airplane (there seem to be almost as many different systems of luggage compartments in the front of the plane as there are aircraft). Once the passengers have cleared the young person separating the two pieces of paper, they then must wait while the people ahead of them struggle with varying degrees of success to stuff their oddly shaped luggage into compartments that are supposed to receive them—and after the first ten passengers, there really isn't room.

The net result is something like a half-hour late departure for any crowded flight and enormously frazzled nerves for passengers and flight attendants alike. The paper detachment and luggage disposal problems have been with the airlines since the beginning. There is no reason to think that they will ever be solved.

2) All over the country the large hotel chains have erected high-rise slums of the public housing variety, masquerading as luxury hotels. These high-rise slums are nothing more than layers of cheap motel rooms with neurotic telephone systems, inadequate elevators, incompetent room service and housekeepers who no longer believe "Do Not Disturb" signs. Moreover, they have not yet solved the problems of check-in and check-out time. One can wait as long as a half hour to claim one's reservation. The other morning, in a certain high-rise hotel slum, I counted twenty-three people standing in line to check out. Computers have been introduced, but all they do is print neater bills. Those who check out the hotel's guests are exactly the opposite of the flight attendant at the airplane entrances: They must staple these pieces of paper together.

The life expectancy of such steel and cement structures is probably less than ten years, and it would probably cost as much to rehabilitate them as to construct new ones, especially if there were any way to repair the shoddy workmanship that went into them in the first place. However, they may be used by the end of the 1980s as places to intern illegal immigrants or welfare recipients.

3) There is one hotel in a Texas city that has deliberately and consciously set out to imitate an elite English hotel on a Texas-size scale. The result is a massive mausoleum in which virtually every detail has been authentically

duplicated. It is a truly impressive phenomenon until you realize that you are in Texas.

4) There may be depression and inflation going on at the same time in the United States and the economy is undoubtedly causing severe hardship for many people, but shopping plazas continue to proliferate and swarms of people seem to be in them every hour of the day and night.

5) All teenage girls in the aforementioned shopping plazas look exactly alike and chew their gum exactly the same way.

6) I never noticed it before, but Chicago is clearly the most beautiful city in the country and becomes môre beautiful with each passing year. Heaven knows, we don't deserve it and it may not last, but it should be enjoyed while it lasts. There was, after all, a time when the Cubs won pennants and the Bears national football championships. But that was a long time ago—back when there were no major football or baseball teams in Texas —and precious few Yankees, either.

Commitment
in Fashion Again

Commitments, it would seem, are back in—at least cautious commitments from which you can always get out. Psychologist Maxine Schnall, in her book *Limits: A Search for Values* argues that the limits we impose on ourselves when we make and keep commitments are the way we find values.

In the sixties, Ms. Schnall tells us the things that were "in" were keeping your options open, instant gratification, novelty and excitement, openness to experience, feeling and perceiving, spontaneity, lack of moral restraint, self-centeredness, pleasurable activity and living for the moment.

Now in the eighties, she argues, the fashionable behaviors are commitment, discipline, loyalty, responsibility, rational thought, structure, guilt, obligations to others, hard work and concern about the future.

I'm skeptical about such thematic treatment of decades, such simplistic opposition of behaviors which can often be combined and generalizations which apply much more to the elite than to everyone. Yet I'm prepared to agree with Ms. Schnall that—at a broad level of generalization—she has caught the spirit of a major and glacial social change that is taking place.

Yet *Limits* is a curious book. Early on, the author ridicules mercilessly the fashion of "romantic divorce," yet toward the book's end she describes her own divorce in the very terms that she criticizes. *Limits* apparently means that others have to keep their commitments, no matter what, but you don't have to keep yours, not if you think you have a good reason for not living up to your promises.

I confess that I am appalled by the ease with which people shed commitments in our time, whether it be to marriage or the priesthood or friendship. I was raised to believe that you stood by your vows, kept your word, honored your promises and did not violate commitments. Yet it seems in the years since 1965 that a commitment has no currency value at all. It—and the required astronomic fare—can get you a ride on the local mass transit system of your choice.

I can see two grounds for releasing someone from a commitment: Immaturity about the nature of the decision, deep-down immaturity, and ignorance about what was involved in the commitment, fundamental and basic ignorance. These are the grounds on which the Roman Catholic Church currently annuls marriages and dispenses priests from their vows, and I think that if the church is going to be in the business of annulments and dispensations (which is problematic in my mind), such are indeed valid grounds.

Or to put the matter less legalistically, I would argue that a commitment is only a commitment if it involves an overwhelming presumption of its validity on the part of both the one who makes it and the one(s) to whom it is made.

I don't want to make commitments absolutely irrevocable. I do want to see the presumption in favor of them, instead of against them, as seems to have been the case in the last two decades. Sometimes I have the impression that many people left the priesthood or reneged on their marriage commitments because it was the thing to do and everyone was doing it. I make no judgments about individual cases because that's God's job, not mine. Yet it is hard to escape the impression that there was a mood in society that said you were only really free when you'd violated a fair number of your fundamental commitments.

Men and women may now realize that you cannot live a fully human life unless you and others are normally held to their commitments (held not by law but by such old-fashioned concepts as honor and integrity and character). Yet it seems that the attitude now is that others have to keep their commitments but I don't have to keep mine, others have to impose limits on themselves but I need not, others have to be loyal, but I'm dispensed from loyalty.

So if the seventies were the "me" decade, it would appear that the eighties are on their way to becoming the "me but not them" decade.

I can't quite see that as progress.

Why Not Fire Bradlee as Well as Janet Cooke?

There is a certain poetic justice of the "chickens coming home to roost" variety in the Washington *Post*'s blunder of nominating for a Pulitzer Prize a story that was as fake as the Nixon Watergate cover-up. The *Post* is in great part responsible for the emergence of a new kind of young reporter in American journalism—ambitious, ruthless and utterly without principle or integrity.

One wonders why Janet Cooke, the young woman who faked the story about the child heroin addict in Washington, was fired and Ben Bradlee, the editor, who was taken in by it and defended Ms. Cooke from the legitimate protests of the Washington city government, was not fired.

If Mr. Nixon was responsible for the overzealous invaders of the Watergate complex, why is Mr. Bradlee not responsible for an overzealous reporter who made up a good story because she was unable to find one that was good enough in the real world?

All the President's Men persuaded many young reporters that they too could become folk heroes if they were tough enough, clever enough and tricky enough. Adversary investigative journalism was the new "big game" promising high stakes to the winners. Woodward and Bernstein played it clean in their White House investigation (subsequent work by Woodward and Scott Armstrong on the Supreme Court certainly involved persuading young court clerks to behave dishonorably). The *Post* cannot be blamed for launching adversary investigative reporting as a national pastime. It can be blamed for not realizing the dangers involved in not watching very carefully the abuses that were bound to creep into such a chancy profession. Anyone who has had contact with young journalists recently knows that many of them are both amoral and unprofessional and have even adopted the mannerisms of Dustin Hoffman and Robert Redford.

The *Post* acted responsibly in the Watergate case—and bravely too. It did not act responsibly in its failure to realize how easily younger reporters could go beyond the fine line that Woodward and Bernstein walked.

You say that is demanding a lot of the Washington *Post?* No more, I would argue, than the *Post* demands of those it investigates.

I have been stung by two young reporters in recent months. One defended clearly unethical behavior on the grounds that I was a success and therefore it was legitimate to bring me down. I'm not a success, but what kind of journalistic ethics are involved in such an argument? (He didn't bring me down either, but that's another story for which you will have to read my memoirs.)

Another young reporter, doing an exposé for the Arizona *Star* of overpaid and pampered research scholars at the University of Arizona, charged that as a Jesuit priest I was overpaid, even though I did not teach enough and by implication was a researcher rather than a teacher. The truth was that my salary and obligations—teaching, dissertation directing, committee work, examination participation, etc.—are exactly the same as any other senior sociologist of my rank. The only reason for singling me out was that he could throw in the nice little line about "Jesuit priest" that was bound to catch reader attention. At no point did this young "investigative reporter" ever interview me. I could have at least told him that I wasn't a Jesuit.

My abilities as a teacher, reported by anonymous evaluations of students, are a matter of public record at the University of Arizona (a record of which I am, by the way, very proud). The guy from the Arizona *Star* didn't bother to check them.

It's a vest-pocket, highly personal example of which the Washington *Post* scandal is a national example: Young reporters will behave ruthlessly, dishonestly and unprofessionally as long as men like Bradlee let them get away with it. The Washington *Post*'s apology is locking the barn door after the horse escapes.

It differs from Mr. Nixon's Watergate behavior only in that he never apologized.

Stephen King's Horror
Has a
Healing Power

It is very easy to be upset with horror writer Stephen King, for not only has he turned out his annual, successful terrifier, he has also produced a remarkable nonfiction work in which he discusses the meaning and the appeal of the horror story. If you want to appreciate the full range of Mr. King's talents, read

Cujo to be horrified and *Danse Macabre* to understand why you were horrified.

The former is a real blood-chiller with a little bit of the supernatural scariness that has marked such earlier works as *The Shining* and *Carrie*. But most of the terror comes from something that is quite "natural": A wonderfully loving and friendly St. Bernard dog. The dog follows a rabbit into a hole in the ground where he is bitten by rabid bats and then proceeds to destroy four people, including the father of the family to which he belongs and an adoring four-year-old boy. Mr. King makes this gruesome story come alive with a strange mixture of frightfulness and poignancy.

But I ask myself as I write these lines and the reader doubtless asks as he reads them, why read a book about a rabid dog who unintentionally destroys relatively innocent humans? Isn't there enough ugliness in the world?

Yet we devour Mr. King. We shiver as Carrie obliterates her high school graduation class and as the fire-starter wipes out half of the Central Intelligence Agency and as the woman in *Cujo* beats the St. Bernard dog to death, trying unsuccessfully to save the life of the little boy. What kind of ghouls are we?

Mr. King's answer is ingenious and, I believe, persuasive. If I may simplify and paraphrase him, he believes we are all only too well aware of the secret terrors that hide just beneath the surface of everyday life. We may not quite be surrounded by vampires as the people in *Salem's Lot*, but we know that there are evil and destructive forces, at least as deadly as vampires, and more pervasive than rabid dogs, which can easily do us in. We delight not so much in reminding ourselves that the terrors exist as we do in reassuring ourselves that we are capable for the moment of surviving them. Our fascination by the horror story, suggests Mr. King, is because in reading the story we are reassured that there is hope that we may continue to survive the forces of evil a little bit longer.

Unlike some other horror writers who lack his talents and sensitivity, Stephen King never ends his stories with any cheap or easy hope. People are badly hurt, they suffer and some of them die, but others survive the struggle and manage to grow. The powers of evil have not yet done them in. It is little enough, but it is all there is, Mr. King seems to be saying. The mother and father in *Cujo* have lost their four-year-old, but as the book ends they seem to be finding one another. In this respect, at any rate, the horror story is profoundly religious. It celebrates sometimes only tiny smidgens of hope, but hope, like goodness and love, needs only to exist to finally win.

Benedictions for April 1

Hey, have a nice April Fools' Day!

This phrase will make the language prigs in the audience, either on their own initiative or in imitation of such official national language prigs as columnist William Safire or TV reporter Edwin Newman, writhe. "Have a nice day" is out, it's a linguistic "no-no," almost a breach of good breeding. You display inexcusable commonness and vulgarity if you say it.

I'm not altogether sure why, except that it is a favorite of the bubblegum-chewing teenage women who work in the fast-food joints of our country. The language prigs, who ought not to be in the fast-food joints in the first place, surely would not want to be caught in the same category of human beings as bubble-blowing adolescent females.

In fact, like most language forms that end human interaction, "Have a nice day" is a benediction, a blessing. I take my blessings where I can find them, even from teenagers. Maybe I should say especially from teenagers.

"Farewell," for example, means "May you fare well on your journey." And "goodbye" is a wish for about the same thing. We humans don't like to end our interaction interludes (the distaff of the Irish ethnic group seem constitutionally incapable of breaking away from a door), and a blessing, a wishing of well, is a smooth and satisfying way to break off a contact.

I admit that "Have a nice day" is not all that creative or poetic a benediction. The Celts, who abhorred in both their pagan and Christian manifestations abrupt departure (their language lacks words for such situations) devised a whole series of complex blessings to bridge the awkwardness of leave-taking.

Thus one might say upon departing a house, "May Jesus and Mary be with this house."

And the householder would respond, "May Jesus and Mary and Patrick go with you."

Then one would reply, "May Jesus and Mary and Patrick and Brigid bless you all the day long."

And so on and so on. There are a lot of Irish saints.

These days you could find yourself in a lot of trouble if you used those kinds of blessings—in fast-food joints or anywhere else. So until some genius comes along with a better one, "Have a nice day" must suffice as at least an authentic folk blessing of twentieth-century America. I don't use it myself, preferring such leave-takings as "If I don't see you, I'll see you" . . . a free translation of the French "au revoir." If the language prigs keep knocking it though, I might be constrained to make it my own.

Language prigs drive me up the wall, whether they be the kind of people who write you vicious letters about "who and whom" or folks like Mr. Safire, who, having written speeches for President Nixon, has no right to be priggish about anything. English is a marvelously flexible and free-flowing language. It is easy to use and easy to misuse, precisely because it is a language of ordinary people. The real offenders, it seems to me, are not teenage hamburger provenders but intellectuals who use "genocide" for the American intervention in Vietnam and then lack a word to describe what Hitler did and what the Khmer Rouge did once we abandoned Cambodia.

Obviously there have to be rules of language usage, but I much prefer the rules that flow from the ordinary conversation of people to the rules that are made up in academic ivory towers. (An excellent book of rules, by the way, is *Style* written by University of Chicago Professor Joseph Williams. Anyone who writes for a living ought to review it periodically.)

Even bureaucratic jargon—of which Secretary Haig seems to be one of the most skilled creators—has its place, obscuring or hiding the truth sometimes and other times making the trivial sound important. Language doesn't have to communicate ideas on all occasions.

There must be rules and I lament that my teenage friends aren't learning the rules in high school anymore. Like, I mean they're not, *really*. Nonetheless, there also must be a respect for the richness of ordinary speech. "Have a nice day" isn't all that rich as benedictions go, but it's authentic and it represents an honest blessing in an age that doesn't value blessings.

So I'll stick with it.

On April Fools' Day, however, I'll end with a more elaborate blessing. May Patrick, Brigid, Fiona, Kevin, Kathleen and all the rest of them go with you on your journey and may the smile of them be always on your lips . . .

Is One Discrimination Better Than Another?

The young cabdriver was intelligent and good-natured, so we chatted all the way into the Loop from O'Hare International Airport. His name, I noticed from the license, was Islamic, but there were rosary beads on the dashboard. Finally, my curiosity won out and I asked him where he was from. He hesitated and then confessed the terrible truth. He was an Iranian.

Nothing wrong with that, I said. Iran is a great country. We were friends once in the past. We will be friends in the future.

He agreed enthusiastically, but said it was very hard to be an Iranian in America today. His car had been damaged five times and his insurance canceled. Twice within recent months he had been pulled out of his cab and beaten by patriotic Americans. The young man still liked America, and while he wanted to go home to visit his family he was afraid to do so because then he would not be able to finish his education in America. And the rosary beads? Part of his study had been with Polish nuns—"Polish just like the pope." And even though still a Moslem, he also believed in Christianity.

Even though still an Iranian, he also believed in America.

A Catholic beyond any doubt, a credit both to Iran and to America, to both Christianity and Islam.

So he doesn't have any insurance for his car and he has been beaten up twice in the last couple of months by patriotic Americans. Weep less for the young man whose wit and good spirits are still undaunted. Weep for America where there is a new kind of bigotry, a new group it is all right to hate, a new fashionable prejudice, a new socially sanctioned viciousness.

If the young man was one of the militants who had seized the U.S. Embassy and tortured American citizens, well then, yes, maybe there would be some grounds for pulling him out of his cab and beating him up.

He was not sympathetic with the militants and in any event he hadn't been in Tehran when it happened. He was not guilty for anything he had done; rather he was guilty for who he is. Just like others have been guilty throughout our history because they were Jewish or Catholic or Asian or black. Bigotry doesn't die, it merely reasserts itself in another disguise.

It is precisely the risk of reasserting bigotry in another disguise that makes the so-called reverse discrimination in our society such a terribly dangerous gamble. People are now to be denied jobs for which they are the best qualified because they are, for example, white men. They are to be punished, not for any discrimination in which they have engaged, but for the discrimination by white men long since dead, or by other white males who may still be alive. The victims of reverse discrimination are every bit as innocent as my Iranian cabdriver. They weren't there when it happened and they disapprove of it. They are nonetheless guilty, not because of what they've done but because of who they are. Discrimination that is in fact anti-white or anti-male, as far as I can see, is every bit as unjust as discrimination that is anti-Hispanic or anti-Jewish or anti-Iranian; in every case the individual is made to suffer for the sins of a group in whose membership he has no choice.

Ah, say the advocates of reverse discrimination, but those people who beat up your Iranian cabdriver were bigots. We, however, have good intentions. Our ends are to undo social wrongs of the past.

Funny thing, but those who beat up the Iranian cabdriver

would have said that they had good ends too. They intended to avenge the evil done to Americans in Tehran.

The Jesuits never did teach that the ends justified the means. Yet the concept of group guilt, whether it's practiced by Nazis or the Stern gang or the terrorists of the PLO or the IRA or by the Equal Employment Opportunity Commission or by the brutes that beat up my Iranian cabdriver, is the same immorality no matter who is practicing it and for what end.

So-called "liberals" who think their variety of group guilt can be justified by good intentions contribute more than their share of the cultural climate in which innocent young men can be pulled from the cabs and beaten virtually unconscious because they happen to have been born in one of the places where human civilization began.

Few Americans Have
Real Friendships

Friendship has a hard time in America. Most men don't have any male friends at all. Women are more likely to have some friends of their own sex, but womanly friendships are frequently blighted by distrust and a sense of betrayal. Cross-sex friendships outside of marriage are rare either because they quickly turn sexual or because the partners are afraid they will turn sexual, and only a minority of Americans consider their spouse to have the qualities appropriate for a good friend.

Such are the melancholy conclusions of a study by Joel Block (called *Friendship* and published by Macmillan). Dr. Block's study is useful and perceptive. It confirms, however, what many of us have sensed for a long time: Despite all the good things about American culture, it is not conducive to development of friendships.

Men are too busy competing with one another for success to form friendships. Women are too busy competing with each other for men to thoroughly trust one another. Husbands and wives are too busy with the demands of their respective lives to be able to devote the time and the attention necessary to cultivating friendship in marriage. And the propensity to exploit other human beings that is at the root of competitiveness makes cross-sex friendships likely to generate into sexual exploitation— even though in other societies boys and girls can form friendships in childhood that persist for the rest of their lives and are never confused with love affairs.

One of Block's male respondents described poignantly what might almost be called a paradigm of male friendships in American society; a paradigm which with some modification could be applied to other friendship relationships too. "We had a reasonably good time . . . but there was a definite feeling of competition between us. Every encounter became a contest which I felt I had to win or at least hold my own. The major area for the contest was who had the best catch each day. There was also a certain amount of rivalry over preparing food and building the fire in the cabin . . . I felt like a kid back in grade school . . . Like most little boys I was taught that I must compete, that I must be aggressive. I must not be weak, not let on to feelings of weakness, tenderness or dependence, particularly on other men. My parents, relatives, my older brother, all taught me that my self-worth depended on my manliness, my willingness to fight like a man. This lesson was reinforced everywhere—my teachers, the books I read, the movies I saw, all presented an unquestioned definition of male identity."

That is, I think, a fair description of how we raise boys to be men in our society. Too intimate a friendship with another man is a sign minimally of weakness and quite possibly of "even worse." Hispanic Americans are much more open to friendships with other men but as they become middle and upper middle class they seem prone to adopt our pattern of competitiveness and to leave behind the close male friendships that are so much part of the Hispanic culture—despite the machismo which involves all kinds of different but equally serious cultural problems.

So I put it to you, gentle reader-persons. How many of you can claim even one satisfying, trusting, secure friendship, either with a member of your own sex or with a member of the opposite sex, your spouse or someone else? Some Americans can legitimately claim such friendships. We are not a society utterly bereft of friendliness. Yet most of us, it is much to be feared, are so used to a life without deep friendships that we take it for granted, assume that it is normal and natural, and indeed become suspicious of those who apparently do have friends.

For men, it is the worst of all. Barred from friendships with other men, too busy and perhaps too frightened to become friends with their wives, threatened by friendships with other women, American men seem doomed to lives of loneliness and isolation. Small wonder that their life expectancies are so much lower than those of their wives and sisters. Priests, bizarrely enough, seem to be better off than most other men, for they are to some extent out of the competitive race and sexually more or less safe (less now than in ages past), and hence both men and women can have friendships with them somewhat more readily. Obviously, however, the solution to the American friendship problem is not to ordain everyone a priest.

But there is no obvious solution other than a massive cultural realignment that denies the identification of strength with rugged individualistic competitiveness; an identification that is the core of our patriarchal culture and that is strongly endorsed by much of the feminist movement, which sees equality to be achieved for women through their becoming as competitive as men are.

It is not a problem, however, for which a solution can be long delayed, for more and more Americans are desperately looking for affection and support and no matter where they look they can't find it.

Mass Transit Shootout

The trouble with Tombstone was not that it was lawless, but that it had too much law. This is the trouble with most American cities.

As the one-hundredth anniversary of the famous gunfight at the OK Corral (which really wasn't fought at the OK Corral) draws near, my colleague, Professor James Harkin, is doing a serious analysis of Tombstone in the time of the Earps and the Clantons as a problem of public administration. Everyone who participated in the famous gunfight, he notes, was a lawman of one sort or another. For all its violence, Tombstone was filled with law officers. Much of the violence, like the brief shootout between the Earps and the Clantons, involved one law enforcement officer shooting at another.

Tombstone has become a myth of American life, not because it was so very different from the rest of the country, but because it was so very similar. Conflicting jurisdictions, responsibilities and politics brought the Earps, Doc Holliday, the Clantons and the McLowerys to their shootout. The same sort of conflicting jurisdictions and responsibilities are responsible for the mass transit problems in Chicago, New York and Boston, and most of the fiscal woes that assail America's big cities. When Mayor Ed Koch and Governor Hugh Carey, Mayor Kevin White and Governor Ed King, Mayor Jane Byrne and Governor James Thompson fight it out in the contemporary equivalent of the OK Corral, they are caught in the same kind of pressures and react with the same kind of shoot-from-the-hip style as did Ike Clanton and Doc Holliday.

The Earp crowd represented the city interests of Tombstone. The Clantons and their ally, Sheriff John E. Behan, represented the county. The Earps were Republicans, with the federal government vaguely behind them. The Clantons were Democrats with the old Tombstone power structure behind them. (To this day, they will tell you in Tombstone that the Clantons were the good guys and the Earps were the bad guys.) Both sides had their law on their side—so much so that "Marshal" Wyatt Earp had eventually to flee Tombstone lest he be arrested by the law (the "other" law) and tried for murder.

When everyone has power no one has power, and when the responsibility is divided, no one has responsibility. The cities of Chicago, New York and Boston are responsible for keeping public transportation running. So are the states of Illinois, New York and Massachusetts. So are the three respective transit authorities. When transit collapses in many of the cities, who is to blame? The mayor? The governor? The chairman of the transit authority? Take your pick and then head for the OK Corral to cheer for your favorite.

No one wants to assume responsibility for raising transportation costs (inflation may affect other costs, but it's not supposed to affect subway fares). Neither the city nor the transportation authority has the fiscal and taxing power to subsidize public transportation, and the out-of-city legislators who control the state purse strings don't see why they should come up with the money (even if the money happens to have been gathered by taxing those who live in the cities). If there was one governmental authority with the clear responsibility and clear power to maintain public transportation, the alarms and the excursions, the heaving and the tugging, the shouting and the mock shootouts would never occur.

But we Americans have so devoured power in our big cities that there are too many responsibilities and too many politicians. Important and difficult decisions don't get made and public services drift from crisis to crisis. Now that the Reagan administration has, in effect, abandoned cities, crises like those that affect New York and Chicago are going to be routine.

And a smart urban mayor will begin to look for a modern equivalent of Doc Holliday.

The August Hate Meter
Turns Maroon

"Well, it's August," said a very perceptive friend of mine, "and the hate meter is turning maroon."

He was describing the volatile emotions of a summer-home community as the vacation weeks wind down. It could have been any summer community in the Western world, and the strains of late August in a resort neighborhood tell a lot about the peculiarities of upper-middle-class family life.

In almost any vacation community, the social structure is bizarre. The women and children flock to the summer homes in late June or early July, leaving behind the city and its problems. Also left behind are the husbands and fathers who appear on weekends, hoping that the inevitable Sunday rainstorm won't wipe out their golf game.

So much is taken for granted in this partial separation of the family through the summer months, it is rarely asked whether this odd custom (by the standards of other cultures, at any rate) is healthy for husbands or wives, parents or children, indeed for anyone but the celibate scholar and writer who likes to water-ski and who exults in a virtually limitless supply of teenagers who will do almost anything to be invited to ski.

It is not good for women to be deprived of their men for five days of the week. Nor is it good for men to be deprived of their women. The physical and psychological tensions that build up in such "bachelor" lives make the two days when the family is united a touchy and thin-tempered interlude in which both the husband and wife expect extra points because of the sacrifices they have made—the husband enduring the loneliness of an empty house or apartment in the city and the wife enduring the madness of children and dogs running pretty much out of control.

By August everyone is angry at spouses, neighbors and friends, even though the appearance of summer fun must be stoutly maintained. Then the hate meter turns pink, then maroon and by Labor Day flaming crimson.

As a rough rule of thumb, the strain of the dual family existence decreases in direct proportion to the length of the husband/ father's long weekends. If he manages to sleep in the summer home four nights out of seven, the system may work; indeed, it may even be constructive. Three nights out of seven and they have trouble. Two nights out of seven and the family better make sure that its hate meter is in good repair.

OK. So why do they do it? My informal survey this summer would indicate that the most frequent answer is that they do it for the children, just as their parents before them did it for them when they were children. But does it help the children to be separated from their fathers for most of the week and to live in an environment of emotional tension caused by women not having their husbands for five days of the week and the husband's obligation to "catch up" on his various family responsibilities and privileges over the weekend?

That is a question that is not asked and that you do not become very popular for when you try to ask it. If inconvenience and very considerable sacrifice can be justified in the name of doing good for the children, upper-middle-class parents seem not to care what harm is done to their personalities or their own relationships. Should one say to them, "Hey, you ought to think about your own happiness, your own satisfaction, your own piece of mind, your own fulfillment," they look at you as if you had large holes in your head beyond the appropriate number.

Then you say to them that it is not good for children to have a mother who is a weeklong crab and a father who is a weekend grouch because they are trying to do something that is so difficult as to be unnatural. They simply repeat that there is no sacrifice too great if it is for the good of the children.

Under such circumstances there is no point in contending that sometimes sacrifice should be sacrificed so that children can have the biggest advantage of all—happy parents who are happily related to one another.

What then should be done about summer-home communities? The most drastic strategy would be to sell and get out. A more modest strategy is longer long weekends. Our society can probably get along nicely with three-day work weeks during the summer for most of its citizens. A yet more modest strategy is for the husband/father to realize that the best thing he can do for his wife and family is to spend a month with them when he doesn't have to dash off to work in the morning (or in the case of two-career families both parents might spend the month with kids). During such a month the husband/father (and wife/mother in a two-career family) might actually learn to play again as they did when they were kids.

What month? August, of course. And throw the hate meters away.